A COMMITMENT TO GROWTH

A COMMITMENT TO GROWTH
Essays on Education

Geoff Masters

Published in 2025 by Amba Press, Melbourne, Australia
www.ambapress.com.au

First published in 2018 by ACER Press, an imprint of
Australian Council for Educational Research Ltd

© 2025 Geoff Masters

This book is copyright. All rights reserved. Except under the conditions described in the Copyright Act 1968 of Australia and subsequent amendments, and any exceptions permitted under the current statutory licence scheme administered by Copyright Agency Limited (www.copyright.com.au), no part of this publication may be reproduced, stored in a retrieval system, transmitted, broadcast or communicated in any form or by any means, optical, digital, electronic, mechanical, photocopying, recording or otherwise, without the written permission of the publisher.

Text design and typesetting by Peter Long.
Cover image © N Nehring /Tree rings, used under license from Getty Images

ISBN: 9781923569348 (pbk)
ISBN: 9781923569355 (ebk)

A catalogue record for this book is available from the National Library of Australia.

Contents

Foreword — vii
Introduction — x

PART 1: 'BIG FIVE' CHALLENGES IN SCHOOL EDUCATION — 1

Chapter 1: 'Big five' challenges in school education — 2

Chapter 2: Raising the professional status of teaching — 10

Chapter 3: Reducing disparities between Australian schools — 17

Chapter 4: A 21st century curriculum — 24

Chapter 5: The 'long tail' of underachievement — 32

Chapter 6: Getting all children off to a good start — 39

PART 2: IS SCHOOL REFORM WORKING? — 45

Chapter 7: Is school reform working? — 46

Chapter 8: 20-year slide in maths and science learning — 50

Chapter 9: Planning a stronger teacher workforce — 53

Chapter 10: Incentives – an ineffective school improvement strategy — 57

Chapter 11: Focus on the larger purpose of schooling and improvement may follow — 61

Chapter 12: Achievement gaps – the continuing challenge — 63

PART 3: RECONCEPTUALISING EDUCATIONAL ASSESSMENT   67

Chapter 13: Repurposing assessment   68

Chapter 14: Rethinking formative and summative assessment   74

Chapter 15: Challenging our most able students   78

Chapter 16: Monitoring student growth   84

Chapter 17: Towards a growth mindset in assessment   90

Chapter 18: The power of expectation   95

Chapter 19: Learning assessments – designing the future   97

PART 4: SCHOOLS AS LEARNING ORGANISATIONS   103

Chapter 20: Schools as learning organisations   104

Chapter 21: National School Improvement Tool   110

Chapter 22: Essential teaching practices – do they exist?   115

Chapter 23: Learning from mistakes   121

Chapter 24: The hard work of improvement   125

Chapter 25: Addressing the challenges   129

References   134
Index   138

Foreword

How remarkable was Geoff Masters' observation in his 2013 Australian Education Review *Reforming Educational Assessment: Imperatives, principles and practices* that the key to reform lay in conceptualising learning as progress. It is difficult to imagine a teacher who did not conceive of learning in this way. The need to reconceptualise educational assessment reveals the extent to which assessment had become divorced from the purpose of the education it was intended to serve.

The editors of this book have provided a great service in drawing together Masters' writings over the period 2011-2018. This collection shows Masters' willingness to address a wide audience, from academics and researchers to practising teachers, and the accessible style in which he does so.

Masters is not constrained by his own internationally recognised expertise in educational assessment and contemporary psychometric methods. He paints on an encouragingly wide canvas. His chapters in this book begin with his nomination of what he calls the 'big five' challenges in school education. The list is not novel – but the incisiveness and clarity of Masters' analysis and his deft use of data are.

Masters knows from the data on student achievement just how diverse the students at any year level can be, observing that 'the most advanced students commencing any year of school are typically five to six years ahead of the least advanced students' (p. 7). He points out that both whole-class teaching and curricula organised by year level work against any active accommodation of the differences among students within a class.

The solution that Masters proposes is personalised learning supported by well researched learning progressions. There is much discussion of both strategies in the academic literature and public discourse about education these days, but not yet much success in making personalised learning a reality.

As Chair of the interim National Curriculum Board and its successor, the Australian Curriculum Assessment and Reporting Authority (ACARA) from 2008 to 2015, I had the opportunity to observe at close quarters efforts to underpin the development of the new Australian Curriculum. The development of the new Australian Curriculum provides a useful illustration. The design intention was to focus on learning progressions, but this was much easier in subjects such as mathematics and science than in subjects where the progressions were less well delineated in research and, in some cases, where there were relatively arbitrary decisions about content to be made. In English, a progression was well defined in literacy development but not in the way in which literature might be introduced. In history, there was a relatively clear progression in the skills dimension but an arbitrariness in the selection of topics to be studied. Clearly, more work needs to be done on understanding how learning progressions can inform and underpin the development of curriculum.

The Australian Curriculum is accompanied with observations about the range of achievement levels among students at any given year level, and quotes from Masters' *Reforming Educational Assessment* in making these observations, urging that the range of achievement levels be taken into account by using the curriculum as a specification of developmental progressions on which students' learning can be planned and supported.

Is exhortation enough to support personalised learning? A curriculum with a developmental perspective can be undermined by the imposition of an expectation of a common rate of development among students across the years of schooling, as Masters points out:

> Although there is a place for explicit year-level expectations, it is incumbent on education systems and governments to promote practices that do not define success only as the achievement of year-level expectations. (p. 72)

Masters argues that the whole focus of schooling should be on individual students' growth, not on their current state of achievement. He says that abandoning the current A to E grades that report students' individual achievement against year-level curriculum expectations would be an important step in achieving this shift in focus (pp. 82–3).

Such a change would remove some of the clutter, but more is needed to facilitate a full shift in focus to personalised teaching and learning. Good assessment tools, which teachers can use to assess students' current level of progress, can inform decisions about individual students' next learning steps. Masters and the Australian Council for Educational Research are already satisfying some of this need.

However, that may still not be enough. Australian school education might require serious provocation. Would we dare take all year-level expectations off the curriculum documents – and focus instead on promoting progress for every learner? How might teaching practices be transformed? Would parents and the community accept such a radical change? Or would they instead demand that school education retain 'explicit year-level expectations'? Read this book with these questions in mind.

Emeritus Professor Barry McGaw AO
University of Melbourne

Introduction

In 2013, Professor Geoff Masters, Chief Executive Officer of the Australian Council for Educational Research (ACER) and respected international expert on assessment and school improvement, published what was to become a highly influential paper as part of the Australian Education Review series. *Reforming Educational Assessment: Imperatives, principles and challenges (AER 57)* drew on decades of work by Masters and others at ACER and internationally supporting the efforts of national governments, education authorities and local school leaders and teachers to use evidence of student achievement and school and system performance to improve learning outcomes for students.

At a time when governments and systems were increasingly focused on rankings, targets and accountability measures, Masters made a number of important points. Firstly, he argued that while the field of educational assessment had become somewhat muddied over preceding decades, expert opinion was converging on what he called 'a simple unifying principle':

> the fundamental purpose of assessment is to establish where learners are in their learning at the time of assessment

Underpinning this principle is a conceptualisation of learning as progress; the purpose of educational assessment is to understand where learners are in their long-term learning and the progress they are making.

While notionally simple, in drawing our attention back to the learner and defining the 'task' of learners as making long-term progress in an area of learning, Masters successfully reset the national discussion about how best to improve learning outcomes.

Reforming Educational Assessment: Imperatives, principles and challenges situated reform of educational assessment within a context of increasing demands for better information for decision-making, evolving understandings of human learning (including important points about what the evidence tells us about variability in student learning and achievement and the progressive nature of learning), the growing emphasis on broader life skills and attributes, and the transformational potential of new technologies. Masters described the design principles for what he called a 'learning assessment system', including the need to develop empirically based maps of learning progress in each domain of learning. Finally, Masters made the point that effective reform of educational assessment requires not just incremental changes but fundamental changes in mindset. While seemingly simple, the 'paradigm shift' described in the review has significant implications for practice across educational delivery, cutting across entrenched attitudes, beliefs, practices and processes.

The challenges identified in *Reforming Educational Assessment: Imperatives, principles and challenges* and implications for assessment design, curriculum design and teaching and learning have informed much of the debate within the sector and in the public domain over the past five years, in particular promoting ideas of 'growth' and 'progress' and the understanding that where individual learners are in their long-term learning progress needs to be understood and addressed individually and not seen through the 'lock step' of age or grade.

The *Review to Achieve Educational Excellence in Australian Schools*, published five years after *Reforming Educational Assessment* specifically addresses a number of these challenges, adopting the language of growth and individual progress at its core:

> Student growth is a measure of the individual progress a student makes over time along a defined learning progression. Focusing on student growth matters because it enables <u>every</u> student to progress regardless of starting point or capabilities. (*Review*, p. x)

In particular, and strikingly, the *Review* argues strongly for a shift in approach to curriculum design and delivery away from an age- and year-based system to one 'expressed as learning progressions independent of year and age' and underpinned by access to quality assessment tools designed to help teachers 'diagnose a student's current level of knowledge, skill and understanding, to identify the next steps in learning to achieve the next stage in growth, and to track student progress over time against a typical development trajectory.'

The *Review* nails its colours to the mast in terms that echo much of what is argued in this collection:

> Delivering the maximum individual learning growth for every student every year is the key to reversing the decline in Australia's education outcomes. (*Review*, p. x)

This collection of publications by Masters over the period 2011–2018 is an attempt to describe an emerging consensus defining the challenges faced in modern school education and how evidence-based approaches can address these challenges to achieve the ultimate ambition: improved learning outcomes for all students.

Part 1 of this collection, **'Big Five' Challenges in School Education**, focuses on identifying the 'problem' in Australian school education. The challenges identified by Masters include raising the status and attractiveness of teaching as a profession, reducing disparities between schools, designing a curriculum for the 21st century, promoting teaching and learning approaches focused on growth that better meet the needs of individual students, and identifying and meeting the needs of children on trajectories of low achievement.

Part 2, **Is School Reform Working?**, reflects on previous efforts to reform school education and deliver improved outcomes for learners.

Part 3, **Reconceptualising Educational Assessment**, explores the territory of *Reforming Educational Assessment: Imperatives, principles and challenges (AER 57)*. It includes an extract from the influential 2013 paper *Towards a Growth Mindset in Assessment*.

Part 4, **Schools as Learning Organisations**, focuses on the future of school reform and evidence-based approaches to support schools in their goal of continuous improvement. It includes ACER's submission to the *Review to Achieve Educational Excellence in Australian Schools*.

Many of the pieces featured in this collection were originally published online in *Teacher* magazine. Others were published as part of the ACER Policy Insights series. The original, unabridged versions of many of these papers are available in the public domain and details of where to find them are included in the collection.

The editors have drawn on this body of writing by Professor Masters to attempt to tell the story of these past five years. If the beginning of this story was the publication of *Reforming Educational Assessment: Imperatives, principles and challenges (AER 57)*, the release of the *Review to Achieve Educational Excellence in Australian Schools*, might be seen as the end of the beginning. With a greater understanding and emerging consensus of the challenges, implications and needed approaches, the next chapter in the story must focus on what Masters has called 'the hard work of improvement'.

Ralph Saubern
Kate McGough
Editors

Part I

'BIG FIVE' CHALLENGES IN SCHOOL EDUCATION

Although there is much to celebrate about Australia's schools, there are also significant challenges to be recognised and addressed. Over the past 15 years, international studies reveal the equity gap between advantaged and disadvantaged schools in Australia has barely shifted (Thomson et al. 2017). Despite reform efforts, the performances of Australian school students in national and international assessments remain stagnant, or are in decline. That all Australian students in all Australian schools are entitled to an excellent education *(Australian Education Act, 2013)* is without dispute. But progress in identifying and tackling the challenges hindering educational excellence remains slow.

Many of the challenges confronting schools can be individually identified and discussed, yet they are linked in important ways. Individually or collectively, these challenges must be viewed as a much-needed call to action – for parents, students, teachers, school leaders, system leaders, policy makers, governments, and national education agencies.

CHAPTER 1

'Big five' challenges in school education

AUGUST, 2015, TEACHER

There is no shortage of challenges in school education. Some of the biggest challenges we face can appear frustratingly intractable. Despite reform efforts, regular government reviews and ongoing calls for change, progress in addressing our most significant challenges is often slow and solutions continue to elude us.

It's not that we don't know what the challenges are. But their roots sometimes lie largely outside the reach of schools or in deeply entrenched educational processes and structures that are difficult to change. A political response is sometimes to focus instead on low-hanging fruit and quick wins – to make changes at the margins where change seems possible. However, real reform and significant progress in improving the quality and equity of Australian schooling depend on tackling our deepest and most stubborn educational challenges. Here are five such challenges.

Raising the professional status of teaching

A first challenge is to raise the status of teaching as a career choice, to attract more able people into teaching and to develop teaching as a knowledge-based profession.

As Michael Barber and Mona Mourshed (2007) observed in their report, *How the world's best-performing schools come out on top*, the top-performing school systems internationally consistently attract highly able people into teaching, thus driving up the status of the profession and attracting even more able entrants. In high-performing countries such as Singapore and Hong Kong, teachers are drawn from the top 30 per cent of school leavers. In South Korea and Finland, teachers are drawn from the top 10 per cent. In these high-performing countries, places in teacher education programs are limited and competition for entry is intense.

As Pasi Sahlberg (2010) notes in *The secret to Finland's success: educating teachers*, only one in ten applicants is accepted to study to become a primary teacher in Finland.

Attracting the best and brightest school leavers to teaching is only a first step for top-performing nations. They also work to understand the nature of expert teaching and use this understanding to shape initial teacher education programs, coaching and mentoring arrangements and ongoing professional development. Features of these high-performing systems include rigorous teacher education courses and well-developed processes for defining and recognising advanced teaching expertise.

In contrast to top-performing countries, Australia draws its teachers largely from the middle third of school leavers. And there is little evidence that this is about to change. Following recent demand-driven reforms, some universities are admitting larger numbers of teacher education students with increasingly low Year 12 performances – a trend that may continue as the number of teachers required to staff our schools grows over the next decade.

Meeting this first challenge requires an understanding of why teaching is currently not more attractive, what high-performing countries have done to raise the status of teaching, and what strategies are likely to make teaching a more highly regarded profession and sought-after career in Australia.

Reducing disparities between Australian schools

A second challenge is to reduce the disparity between the schooling experiences of students in Australia's most and least advantaged schools.

The OECD's Programme for International Student Assessment (PISA) shows that some countries have been successful both in lifting overall levels of achievement and in reducing differences related to socioeconomic background. Germany, Mexico and Turkey are examples. Two conclusions from recent PISA studies are that increased national performance is associated with greater equity in the distribution of educational resources and that equity can be undermined when school choice segregates students into schools based on socioeconomic background. According to the OECD, at least as important as how much countries spend on schools is how these resources are distributed across schools.

Although Australia performs relatively well in PISA, both in terms of quality and equity, there are trends that should be of concern. These include a steady decline in the average performance of Australian 15-year-olds since 2000 and no reduction in the relationship between student performance and socioeconomic background.

Perhaps even more concerning has been an increase in between-school variance in PISA (a measure of the extent to which Australian schools differ from each other). In Finland, which has a comprehensive school system and little social stratification by location, between-school variance in reading increased from eight per cent to nine per cent between 2000 and 2009. In Australia, as John Ainley and Eveline Gebhardt (2013) observe in their report *Measure for Measure*, between-school variance increased from 18 per cent to 24 per cent, suggesting that our schools became more different from each other over this time. Significant between-school increases also were recorded in New Zealand, Sweden and the United States.

Further, there was a significant increase in the gap between low and high socioeconomic schools in Australia over this period. Australia was the only OECD country to observe such an increase, with several countries recording a significant decrease. And there is little reason for optimism that this trend is about to reverse.

Meeting this second challenge depends on identifying and implementing policies – including school funding policies – capable of reducing disparities between Australia's schools.

Designing a 21st-century curriculum

A third challenge is to re-design the school curriculum to better prepare students for life and work in the 21st century.

Today's world is vastly different from that of 50 years ago. And the pace of change is accelerating, with increasing globalisation; advances in technology, communications and social networking; greatly increased access to information; an explosion of knowledge; and an array of increasingly complex social and environmental issues. The world of work also is undergoing rapid change with greater workforce mobility, growth in knowledge-based work, the emergence of multi-disciplinary work teams engaged in innovation and problem solving, and a much greater requirement for continual workplace learning. The school curriculum must attempt to equip students for this significantly changed and changing world.

However, many features of the school curriculum have been unchanged for decades. We continue to present disciplines largely in isolation from each other, place an emphasis on the mastery of large bodies of factual and procedural knowledge and treat learning as an individual rather than collective activity. This is particularly true in the senior secondary school, which then influences curricula in the earlier years. As a result, students' experiences of school subjects can be very different from the experiences of those who ultimately work in these disciplines, as Jo Boaler (2015) notes in *What's Math Got to Do With It?*, and there is little evidence that these general features of the school curriculum are about to change.

At the same time, we are seeing a decline in the popularity of subjects such as advanced mathematics and science and a decline in the performances of Australian students in comparison with students in some other countries. International studies indicate that the top 10 per cent of our Year 8 students now perform at about the same level in mathematics as the top 50 per cent of students in Singapore, Korea and Chinese Taipei. Again, it is not obvious that we have policies in place to reform mathematics and science curricula in ways that might reverse these trends in subject enrolments and performance.

Meeting this third challenge requires a significant rethink of the school curriculum. Objectives should include giving greater priority to the skills and attributes required for life and work in the 21st century – including skills in communicating, creating, using technologies, working in teams and problem solving – and developing students' deep understandings of essential disciplinary concepts and principles and their ability to apply these understandings to complex, engaging real-world problems.

Promoting flexible learning arrangements focused on growth

A fourth challenge is to provide more flexible learning arrangements in schools to better meet the needs of individual learners.

The organisation of schools and schooling also has been largely unchanged for decades. Although composite classes are common, students tend to be grouped into year levels, by age, and to progress automatically with their age peers from one year of school to the next. A curriculum is developed for each year of school, students are placed in mixed-ability classes, teachers deliver the curriculum for the year level they are teaching, and students are assessed and graded on how well they perform on that curriculum.

This approach to organising teaching and learning might be appropriate if students of the same age commenced each school year at more or less the same point in their learning. But this is far from the case; the most advanced students commencing any year of school are typically five to six years ahead of the least advanced students. In practice this means that less advanced students often struggle with year-level expectations and are judged to be performing poorly – often year after year. At the other extreme, some more advanced students are unchallenged by year-level expectations and receive high grades year after year with minimal effort.

Underpinning this practice is a tacit belief that the same curriculum is appropriate for all, or almost all, students of the same age. Learning success and failure are then defined as success or failure in mastering this common curriculum. This age-based approach to organising teaching and learning is deeply entrenched and reinforced by legislation that requires teachers to judge and grade all students against year-level expectations.

Meeting this fourth challenge depends on more flexible ways of personalising teaching and learning – for example, by using technology to better target individuals' current levels of achievement and learning needs – and on defining learning success and failure in terms of the progress, or growth, that individuals make over time, regardless of their starting points. In this way, excellent progress becomes an expectation of every student, including those who are already more advanced.

Identifying and meeting the needs of children on trajectories of low achievement

A fifth challenge is to identify as early as possible children who are at risk of falling behind in their learning and to address their individual learning needs.

By Year 3, there are wide differences in children's levels of achievement in learning areas such as reading and mathematics. Some children are already well behind year-level expectations, and many of these children remain behind throughout their schooling. They are locked into trajectories of 'underperformance' that often lead to disengagement, poor attendance and early exit from school.

Trajectories of low achievement often begin well before school. Differences by Year 3 tend to be continuations of differences apparent on entry to school when children have widely varying levels of cognitive, language, physical, social and emotional development. Some children are at risk because of developmental delays or special learning needs; some begin school at a disadvantage because of their limited mastery of English or their socioeconomically impoverished living circumstances; and some, including some Indigenous children, experience multiple forms of disadvantage.

Many children in our schools not only remain on trajectories of low achievement, but also fall further behind with each year of school. They make up a long – and sometimes growing – tail of underperforming students, many of whom continually fail to meet minimum standards of achievement. In the 2014 National Assessment Program – Literacy and Numeracy (NAPLAN), 25 per cent of Indigenous children in Year 3 failed to meet the Year 3 national minimum standard in reading, and 30 per cent of Indigenous students in Year 9 failed to meet the Year 9 national minimum standard. There is little evidence that, as a nation, we are doing a better job of reducing the numbers of students on long-term trajectories of low achievement or of reducing the resulting 'tail' of student underperformance.

Meeting this fifth challenge depends on better ways of: identifying children at risk of being locked into trajectories of low achievement at the earliest possible ages; enhancing levels of school readiness; diagnosing learning difficulties upon entry to school; and intervening intensively during the early years of school to address individual learning needs to give as many students as possible the chance of successful ongoing learning.

> Editors' note: In May 2016, Masters published the widely discussed Policy Insights report 'Five challenges in Australian school education', expanding on these five key challenges, drawing on research, and national and international assessment data, within the context of the ambitious goal, set in 2012, by the Australian Government 'for Australia to be placed, by 2025, in the top five highest performing countries based on the performance of school students in reading, mathematics and science' (Australian Education Act 2013).

CHAPTER 2

Raising the professional status of teaching

SEPTEMBER, 2015, *TEACHER*

In my recent *Teacher* article 'Big five challenges in school education' I argue that one of the biggest challenges we face in school education is to raise the status of teaching as a career choice, to attract more able people into teaching and to develop teaching as a knowledge-based profession.

I observe that, in high-performing countries such as Singapore and Hong Kong, teachers are drawn from the top 30 per cent of school leavers. In South Korea and Finland, teachers are drawn from the top 10 per cent. In these high-performing countries, places in teacher education courses are strictly limited and competition for entry is intense.

In Australia, there appears to be an intention on the part of governments that our teachers also should be drawn from the top 30 per cent of school leavers. The 'Accreditation of initial teacher education programs in Australia: standards and procedures' specifies that entrants to initial teacher education should have levels of personal literacy and numeracy 'broadly equivalent to those of the top 30 per cent of the population'.

So to what extent are teachers being drawn from the top 30 per cent of school leavers in Australia?

Part of the answer can be seen in the following graph (Figure 1). The Australian Tertiary Admission Rank (ATAR), despite its shortcomings, is the best indicator we have of overall performance in Year 12. The graph shows that, while the vast majority of Year 12 offers to Science and Engineering courses are made to students with ATARs above 70, fewer than half of Education offers are made to students with ATARs above 70. In this country, we are falling well short of drawing our future teachers from the top 30 per cent of school leavers.

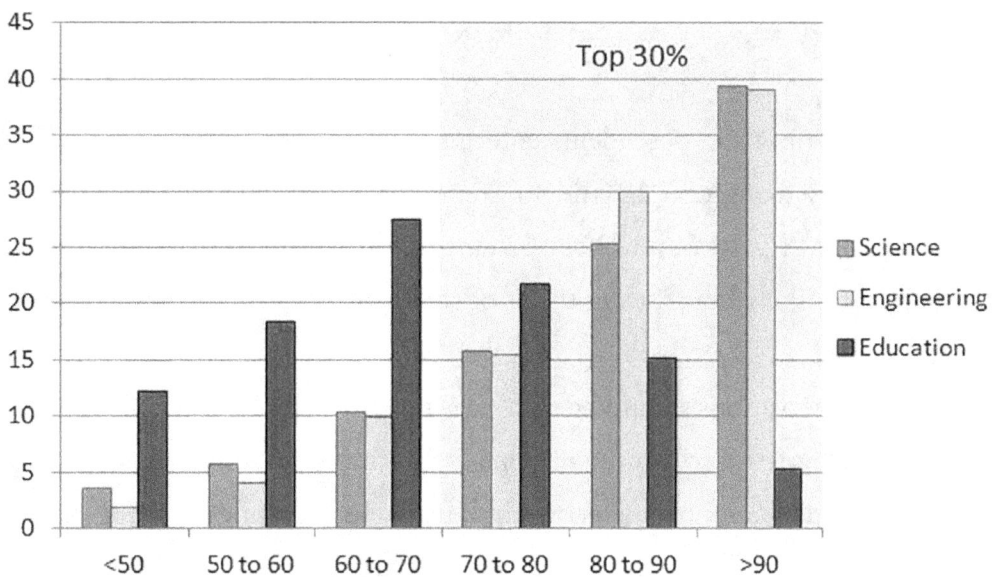

FIGURE 1 Percentage of Year 12 offers in each ATAR band – Science, Engineering and Education (2015)

And the picture is becoming worse, not better. Over the past three years, the percentage of Education offers made to students with ATARs above 70 declined significantly, as shown in Figure 2:

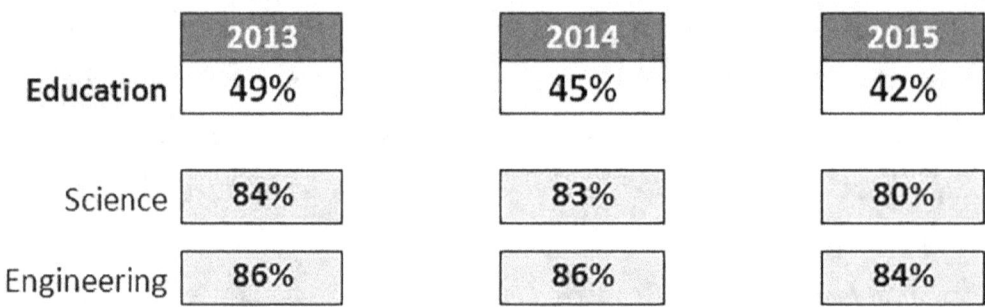

FIGURE 2 Percentage of Year 12 offers to students with ATARs above 70

A large proportion of students entering teacher education courses do not come directly from Year 12 and so are not included in these percentages. However, the ATARs of non-Year 12 entrants are unlikely to be any higher, and are very likely lower, than those of students being made offers directly from Year 12.

These observations should be of concern because the evidence is clear that the world's highest-performing nations in international achievement studies consistently attract more able people into teaching, resulting in better student outcomes. The McKinsey study of the world's best-performing school systems (Barber & Mourshed 2007) found that top-performing countries recruit teachers from the top third of school leavers. That study also concluded that it is not possible to make substantial long-term improvements to a school system without raising the quality of the people entering teaching. There is a clear lesson here for Australia.

A national key performance indicator (KPI)

Given that the world's top-performing school systems recruit the vast majority of their teachers from the top third of school leavers, and Australian governments appear to aspire to do the same, national progress in achieving this goal could be monitored by tracking the percentage of Education offers made to Year 12 students with ATARs greater than 70. This percentage would provide a simple national performance indicator.

This is not to say that ATAR is an ideal measure for selecting teacher education students; some applicants with relatively low ATARs can make excellent teachers. However, very high-performing countries, including Singapore and Finland, place a strong emphasis on academic achievement in their selection processes, and then also select on the basis of other attributes such as motivation for teaching, willingness to learn and communication skills. The high performance of these countries is due in part to deliberate long-term strategies to recruit future teachers from their best and brightest school leavers.

An immediate objective for Australia should be to reverse the downward trend in the percentage of Education offers being made to Year 12 students with ATARs above 70. A short-term objective should be to have *most* Year 12 offers (> 50 per cent) going to students with ATARs above 70. A long-term objective should be to have the *vast majority* of Education offers (e.g. 80 per cent) being made to students with ATARs above 70.

International experience suggests that the achievement of such an objective is entirely feasible. A number of countries have succeeded – usually over a period of time – in making teaching a highly regarded and sought-after career. The ability of these countries to attract more able students into teaching raised the status of teaching, which in turn resulted in still more able students choosing teaching as a career:

> 'Once teaching became a high-status profession, more talented people became teachers, lifting the status of the profession even higher... Where

the profession has a low status, it attracts less talented applicants, pushing the status of the profession down further and, with it, the calibre of people it is able to attract.' (Barber & Mourshed 2007)

In some of the world's highest-performing countries, entry to teaching is now as competitive as entry to courses such as engineering, science, law and medicine.

Effective policies

The construction of a performance indicator to monitor Australia's success in recruiting more able people into teaching is a first step. A second and more important step is to identify policies capable of raising the status of the teaching profession and encouraging more able people to choose teaching as a career. Here, the findings of the McKinsey study are encouraging. That study concluded that, in high-performing countries, improvements in the status of teaching were mainly policy driven; that there are common strategies and best practices for attracting strong candidates into teaching; and that the right policies can change the status of teaching in a country in a relatively short period of time.

According to the McKinsey study, effective policies adopted by these high-performing countries include:

- making teacher education programs highly selective. High-performing countries control entry to teacher education to ensure that the supply of new teachers more or less matches demand. These countries work to ensure that there is not a significant under- or over-supply of graduating teachers. This practice makes teaching more competitive and more highly valued as a career. Limiting the number of students in initial teacher education courses also can result in smaller classes and reduced pressure on professional experience placements

- developing effective student selection processes.
  High-performing countries have well-developed mechanisms for selecting students for entry to initial teacher education. These mechanisms are often multi-step processes involving screening, testing and interviewing applicants. Singapore selects only one in six applicants on the basis of academic results, literacy tests and an interview that considers attitude, aptitude and personality. Finland selects only one in ten applicants using tests of literacy, numeracy, problem solving, critical thinking and information processing, and an interview that considers motivation to teach and learn, communication skills and emotional intelligence

- paying good (but not great) starting salaries.
  High-performing countries pay starting compensation at or above the OECD average. An important consideration appears to be that starting salaries and the salaries of experienced teachers are in line with other professional salaries in the country concerned

- ensuring rigorous initial and continuing professional development.
  High-performing countries establish rigorous initial teacher education courses and set high expectations for teachers' ongoing professional learning. In Finland, policy makers have raised the status of the teaching profession by requiring that all teachers have a master's degree.

Over the past decade, Australia has seen a decline in the performance of our 15-year-olds in the OECD's Programme for International Student Assessment (PISA). At the same time, performances in a number of other countries have improved. Lessons from the world's top-performing nations suggest that a long-term key to reversing Australia's trend will be to make teaching more attractive to the best and brightest of our school leavers, and this, in turn, will depend on a critical set of policy changes.

CHAPTER 3

Reducing disparities between Australian schools

OCTOBER, 2015, *TEACHER*

One of the biggest challenges we face in school education is to reduce current disparities in the schooling experiences of students in Australia's most and least advantaged schools. The general challenge is to ensure that all students receive a high quality education, regardless of where they happen to live or the school that they happen to attend.

This is important because the evidence from the OECD's Programme for International Student Assessment (PISA) is not only that Australian literacy and numeracy levels at 15 years of age have been on a steady decline since the year 2000, but also that disparities between Australian secondary schools have been increasing over this time (Ainley & Gebhardt 2013). Schools in Australia have become increasingly different in their performances in PISA. Associated with this increasing disparity have been increasing differences in performance in low and high socioeconomic status schools.

The opposite has been true in some other countries. A number of countries have achieved significant improvements in national literacy and numeracy levels since 2000, and some countries – including Germany, Mexico and Turkey – have succeeded both in improving overall literacy and numeracy levels and in reducing disparities between schools related to socioeconomic background.

In Australia, evidence from a range of assessment programs reveals significant between-school disparities in student performance. These differences tend to be related to the socioeconomic contexts in which schools operate. For example, the graph in Figure 1 shows average Year 9 NAPLAN reading results for schools grouped according to the Index of Community Socio-Educational Advantage (ICSEA) (Bonnor & Shepherd 2014). The national distribution of Year 9 student results in 2013 is on the right. The graph shows that students in these three ICSEA-based groupings of schools have different average reading levels and gives some indication of the influence of socioeconomic factors on between-school differences in student performance. (Some caution in interpreting the data in Figure 1 is required because of the way in which ICSEA was constructed with reference to NAPLAN results.)

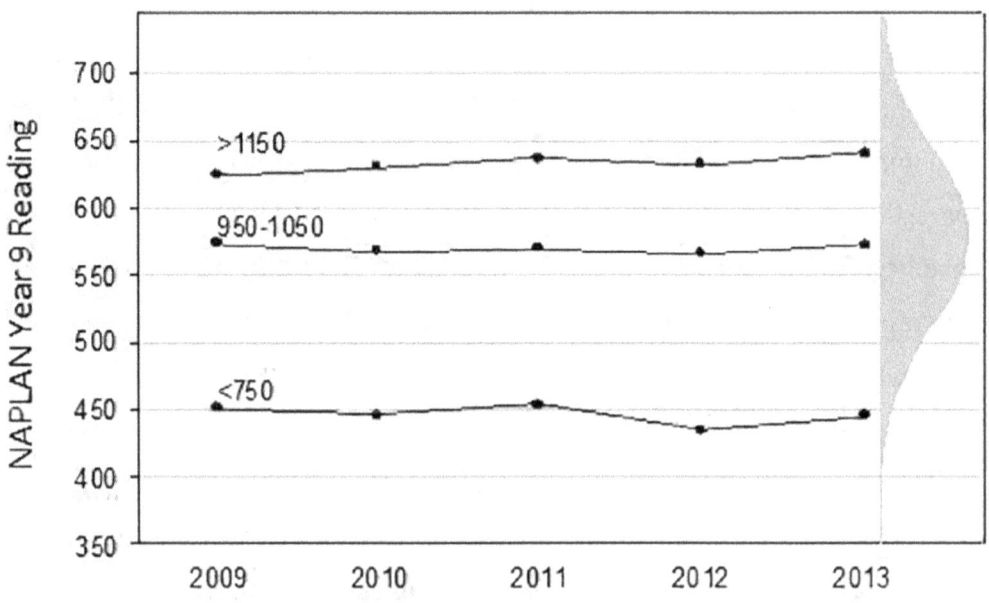

FIGURE 1 Average Year 9 reading results for schools in three ICSEA groups (2009–2013)

Of particular concern is the observation that, since 2000, between-school differences in student performance in PISA have been increasing. In other words, an increasing percentage of the variance in students' levels of performance in Australia is associated with the school they attend. In Finland, between-school variance is relatively low; how students perform is not much associated with the particular school they attend. At the other extreme, in countries that stream students into different kinds of secondary schools (e.g. academic and vocational), between-school variance is much larger than in Australia.

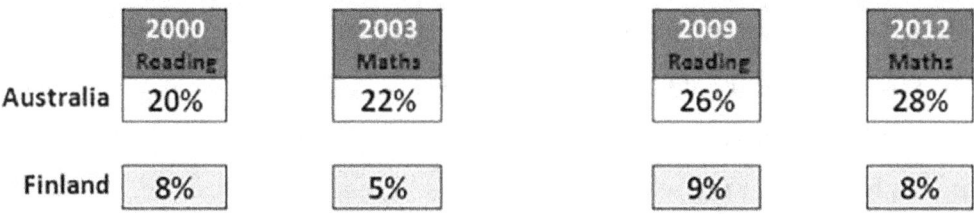

FIGURE 2 Between-school variance as a percentage of total variance (Australia and Finland)

The Australian percentages in Figure 2 may reflect greater between-school differences in mathematics than in reading. Nevertheless, significant increases occurred over these nine-year periods in both reading and mathematics.

A national key performance indicator (KPI)

A straightforward national indicator of disparities between Australian schools is the percentage of total variance in students' performances attributable to 'between-school' differences (with the remaining variance being 'within-school').

An immediate national objective should be to reverse the current trend of increasing disparities between Australian schools as reflected in PISA. A short-term objective should be to reduce between-school differences to levels that existed at the turn of the century. A long-term objective should be to make student outcomes still less dependent on which school they attend, the socioeconomic area in which they live, or school sector.

International experience shows that education policy decisions can either increase or reduce disparities between a nation's schools. For example, since the 1970s, Finland has implemented a comprehensive and fully publicly-funded school system which enrols all children regardless of their socioeconomic background or personal abilities and characteristics (Sahlberg 2007).

There are few private schools, but those that exist are given a government grant comparable to that for state schools and are prohibited from charging tuition fees or making selective admissions. At the other extreme, countries that have adopted policies to stream students into different kinds of secondary schools have created large between-school differences in student performance (between-school variance above 60 per cent). Recently, a number of countries have made policy changes in the face of evidence that overall national performance is associated with reduced disparities between schools.

Effective policies

> Ensuring consistently high standards across schools is a formidable challenge for any school system. Some performance differences between schools may be related to the socioeconomic composition of the school's student population or other characteristics of the student body. School location may also explain differences between schools ... Between-school differences in performance may also be related to the quality of the school or staff or to the education policies implemented in some schools and not in others. (OECD 2013)

In OECD countries generally, a large percentage of between-school variation in student performance is 'explained' by differences in students' and schools' socioeconomic circumstances. In Australia in 2012, 55 per cent of the observed between-school variance in PISA mathematics was associated with differences between schools in average socioeconomic background.

Although between-school differences in student performance are closely associated with socioeconomic status in all OECD countries, some countries have been more successful than others in reducing the impact of socioeconomic disadvantage. Explicit government policies to minimise impact are often at the heart of their success.

Policies for reducing between-school disparities include:

- minimising student residualisation.
  Disparities between a nation's schools are smallest when the student population is distributed evenly across all schools – e.g. when lower performing students or students from poorer socioeconomic backgrounds are not concentrated in particular schools. Government policies are capable of both increasing disparities (e.g. by creating different kinds of schools and streaming students by ability) and reducing disparities (for example, by limiting school fees and prohibiting selective admissions). What a government can realistically do to minimise residualisation will depend on the national context. The important point is that education policies can make a difference to levels of student residualisation and thus to between-school disparities in student outcomes

- maximising access to quality teachers and leaders.
  Disparities between a nation's schools also can be reduced by

ensuring that high-quality teaching and school leadership are more equitably distributed across all schools. To the extent that the most effective teachers and school leaders are concentrated in particular schools, while other schools struggle to recruit and retain highly able teachers and leaders, between-school disparities in student performance are increased. In some education systems, it is not uncommon for less effective teachers and leaders to be moved over time into less 'attractive' schools – usually those that face the biggest challenges and are most in need of high quality teaching and leadership

- promoting effective school improvement practices. Between-school disparities in student performance also are influenced by the extent to which some schools implement more effective day-to-day practices than others. Highly effective practices include creating a school culture of high expectations; setting an explicit and shared school improvement agenda; creating opportunities for teachers to collaborate in evaluating and improving their day-to-day teaching; providing professional learning focused on improved teaching practices; identifying and addressing the needs of individual learners; and monitoring student progress and providing feedback in forms that guide next steps in learning (Masters 2012). Education systems and governments are in strong positions to support all schools in their use of evidence-based practices of these kinds.

Overall levels of national expenditure on schools are generally not highly correlated with measures of student performance or equity. However, there is international evidence to show that how resources are used does make a difference. A conclusion of the OECD is that improvements in national literacy and numeracy levels tend to be associated with the more equitable distribution of resources across schools. When national resources are used to minimise student residualisation, to ensure that every school has access to high quality teaching and school leadership, and to promote the use of effective, evidence-based practices in every school, it is more likely that every student will receive a high quality education regardless of the school they attend.

> Editors' note: Following the publication of this essay, results from the 2016 cycle of the PIRLS (Progress in International Reading Literacy Study) assessment showed that although the literacy achievement of Year 4 Australian students had improved, significant achievement gaps by gender, Indigenous status, socioeconomic status and by school location still remain. Results from PISA 2015 mathematics indicated that 63% (an increase of 8% from PISA 2012) of the performance differences observed across schools can be accounted for by socio-economic background.

CHAPTER 4

A 21st century curriculum

NOVEMBER, 2015, *TEACHER*

In school education, identifying and developing the knowledge, skills and attributes required for life and work in the 21st century is one of the biggest challenges we face. It is an ongoing curriculum challenge.

There are several reasons for questioning how well the current school curriculum is equipping students for life beyond school.

First, there has been a long-term decline in the ability of Australian 15-year-olds to apply what they are learning to everyday problems. This decline is evident in performances in the OECD's Programme for International Student Assessment (PISA). Over the first twelve years of this century, Australian students completed their compulsory study of mathematics and science with declining levels of 'literacy' – that is, declining abilities to apply fundamental concepts and principles in real-world contexts (see Figure 1).

These declines are occurring at a time when literacy levels in a number of other countries are improving and when Australia requires a more literate citizenry. As a nation we require adults who can engage in a discerning way with sophisticated information about a growing number of complex societal and environmental challenges.

Second, we have witnessed a long-term decline in the proportion of Year 12 students choosing to study advanced subjects – especially advanced mathematics and science subjects. For example, the national participation rates in physics and advanced mathematics have been declining steadily for the past two decades (see Figure 2).

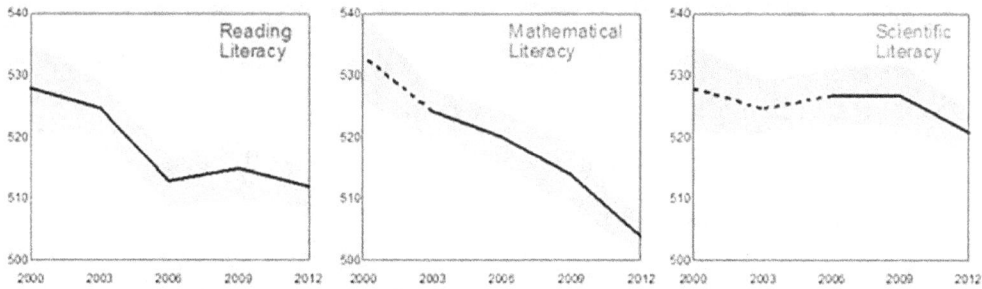

FIGURE 1 Average performance of Australian 15-year-olds in reading, mathematical and scientific literacy (2000–2012)

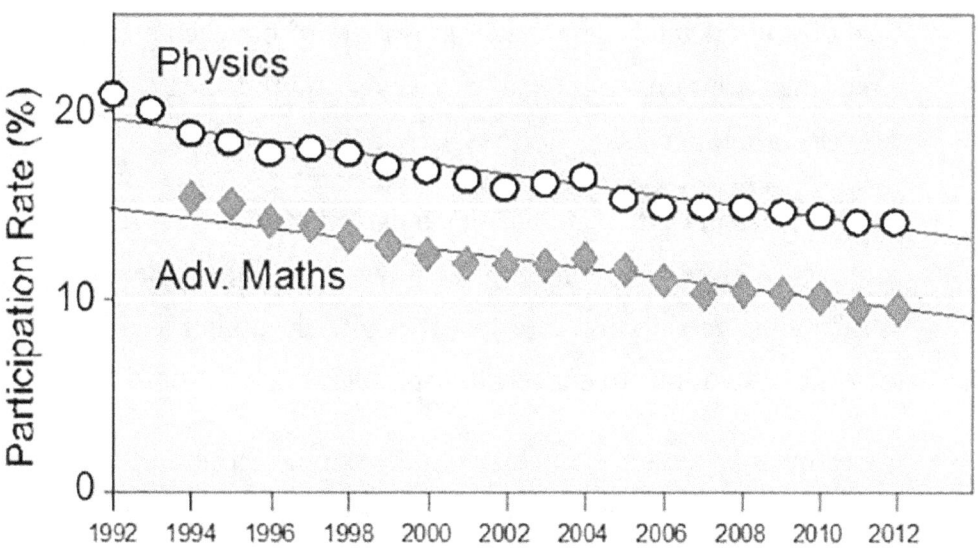

FIGURE 2 National participation rates in Year 12 physics and advanced mathematics (1992–2012)

Again, these declines are occurring at a time when the economy and an increasing number of occupations are requiring graduates with advanced science, technology, engineering and mathematics (STEM) skills. Long-term trends in participation rates raise questions about the future supply of STEM specialists (including mathematics and science teachers) and about the implications for Australia's ability to compete and contribute to international research and advances in these fields.

And there are other reasons for questioning how well the school curriculum is preparing students for life and work in the 21st century:

- Current curricula often are dominated by substantial bodies of factual and procedural knowledge, at a time when it is increasingly important that students can apply deep understandings of key disciplinary concepts and principles to real-world problems.

- School subjects tend to be taught in isolation from each other, at a time when solutions to societal challenges and the nature of work are becoming increasingly cross-disciplinary.

- School curricula often emphasise passive, reproductive learning and the solution of standard problem types, at a time when there is a growing need to promote creativity and the ability to develop innovative solutions to entirely new problems.

- Assessment processes – especially in the senior secondary school – tend to provide information about subject achievement only, at a time when employers are seeking better information about students' abilities to work in teams, use technology, communicate, solve problems and learn on the job.

- Students – especially in the senior secondary school – often learn in isolation and in competition with each other, at a time when workplaces are increasingly being organised around teamwork and are requiring good interpersonal and communication skills.

- School curricula tend to be designed for delivery in traditional classroom settings, at a time when new technologies are transforming how courses are delivered and learning takes place.

Challenges of these kinds will not be addressed by changes to the school curriculum alone. They also depend on investments in teacher quality, changes in pedagogy (how curriculum content is taught) and the alignment of assessment processes to new curriculum priorities. Nevertheless, the content and organisation of the curriculum and the emphases given to different forms of learning in the curriculum are important determinants of student engagement and learning outcomes.

A national key performance indicator (KPI)

Although there is much more to the school curriculum than literacy and numeracy, students' abilities to read and understand different forms of written material and to apply mathematics to everyday problems are among the most important outcomes of an effective curriculum. These are building blocks for many other curriculum areas and essential skills for life and work beyond school. It is for this reason that many countries monitor the literacy levels of 15-year-olds through the OECD's PISA surveys. For Australia, a curriculum challenge is to develop higher levels of these skills by the completion of secondary schooling.

A simple measure of success in achieving this goal is available through PISA. Figure 3 shows changes in Australia's mean reading and mathematical literacy results since 2000. Reading literacy declined by 16 points and mathematical literacy by 29 points over this 12-year period. (Sixteen points and 29 points represent .16 and .29 of the international standard deviation in 2000.) In contrast, the mean reading literacy level in Germany increased by 24 points over the same period. The immediate goal should be to arrest this decline in Australia's performance. The longer-term goal should be to return the performances of Australian students to at least the levels at the turn of the century.

		2000	2003	2006	2009	2012
Australia	Reading Literacy	0	-3	-15	-13	-16
	Mathematical Literacy	0	-9	-13	-19	-29
Germany	Reading Literacy	0	+7	+11	+13	+24

FIGURE 3 Change in mean student performance since 2000 (OECD PISA)

A second indicator of success would be an increase in the percentage of Year 12 students choosing to study advanced STEM subjects. Despite the important of these disciplines in the 21st century, including their relevance to a growing number of occupations, a declining percentage of students are attracted to studying advanced STEM subjects. A significant reversal in current trends may require a radical rethink of the advanced STEM curriculum.

A third indicator would be a measurable increase in the kinds of general skills and attributes now being sought by employers – for example, students' abilities to work in teams, use technology, communicate, solve problems and learn on the job. Currently we lack valid and reliable measures of 'new metrics' of these kinds. A challenge is to develop credible indicators of such capabilities and to use these indicators to evaluate curriculum reform efforts.

Some priorities

A curriculum that prepares students for life and work in the 21st-century is likely to be one that includes an emphasis on:

- deep understandings of subject matter and the ability to apply what is learnt;

- the ability to communicate and solve problems in teams;

- the ability to think critically and to create novel solutions; and

- flexibility, openness to change and a willingness to learn continually.

Here are two specific challenges for a 21st-century curriculum.

Prioritise depth not breadth of learning

The balance between breadth and depth is a fundamental consideration in all curriculum design. Breadth relates to the range or amount of content (often factual and procedural knowledge) covered in the curriculum. Depth relates to the development of deep understandings of key concepts and principles and the ability to apply these understandings in unseen contexts. Ideally, a curriculum would promote both broad and deep learning; in practice, an emphasis on one form of learning often limits opportunities for the other.

For example, school curricula are sometimes described as being 'crowded' with content that teachers are expected to cover. The attempt to provide students with some knowledge about a wide range of topics can lead to 'mile wide, inch deep' curricula that result in superficial learning, incomplete understandings of core concepts and limited ability to transfer and apply knowledge to unfamiliar contexts.

Although the mastery of factual and procedural knowledge is essential in all school subjects, this knowledge must be more than a list of facts and formulas; it must be organised around core concepts or 'big ideas' of the discipline (Bransford et al. 1999). At the present time, the requirement that teachers cover a wide range of curriculum topics often limits the time available to develop deep appreciations of core disciplinary concepts.

Promote cross-disciplinary, team-based problem solving

An important question at any time is how well the school curriculum is preparing students with the knowledge and skills required for life and work beyond school. In the past, the curriculum prepared students with skills and knowledge for a lifetime of work in specific, well-understood occupations. In the 21st century, the curriculum must prepare students for working lives that may span a range of occupations, many of which may not currently exist. An increasing number of students are likely to work in cross-disciplinary teams that form and re-form around emerging challenges, often resulting from advances in digital technologies.

To prepare students for life and work of this kind, the school curriculum needs to include a greater focus on the collaborative solution of real, complex problems. For example, in the senior secondary school, rather than teaching, assessing and reporting student learning only in the context of traditional disciplines, students could be required to work in teams on cross-disciplinary challenges. Through these challenges they could be taught how to apply disciplinary knowledge and understandings in new contexts and assisted to develop skills in working as a team, creating innovative solutions, communicating, solving problems and using technology. Students' work on such projects could be assessed and reported alongside their subject results, providing evidence of a broader range of 21st century skills and attributes.

CHAPTER 5

The 'long tail' of underachievement

FEBRUARY, 2016, *TEACHER*

The fourth 'big challenge' we face as educators is to find better ways to meet the learning needs of the many students who fall behind in our schools, fail to meet year-level expectations (often year after year) and, as a consequence, become increasingly disengaged.

The OECD estimates that approximately 40 000 Australian 15-year-olds (that is, one in seven students) fail to achieve an international baseline proficiency level in reading. After 10 or more years of school, these students lack the reading skills that the OECD believes are required to participate adequately in the workforce and to contribute as productive citizens in the 21st century.

The situation is worse in mathematics where an estimated 57 000 Australian 15-year-olds (that is, one in five students) fail to achieve the international baseline level. At the completion of their compulsory study of mathematics, these students lack the mathematical knowledge and skills judged by the OECD to be adequate for life beyond school.

By international standards, Australia does not have an unusually large percentage of 15-year-olds performing below the international baseline. Some countries have significantly higher percentages. Nevertheless, it is of concern that so many Australian 15-year-olds are failing to achieve minimally adequate levels of reading and mathematical literacy. And it is instructive that a few countries have less than half Australia's percentage of underperformers.

Students who perform below expectation at 15 years of age have generally performed below year-level expectations for much, if not all, of their schooling. They tend to start each school year behind most of their age group and they are poorly equipped for the material they are about to be taught. Most struggle, and this is reflected in their poor performance on the year-level curriculum. Many students receive low grades year after year, reinforcing the message that they are not succeeding at school – or worse, that they are inherently poor learners.

In Australia, as in many other countries, part of the policy response to underachievement has been to set higher standards and to hold students, teachers and schools accountable for achieving those standards. Curricula have been developed that make explicit the standards that all students in each year of school are expected to meet. And we have made it a national requirement that teachers judge and grade students (using A to E or equivalent ratings) on how well they achieve year-level curriculum expectations.

In other words, the policy response has been to confirm existing practice – to set clear curriculum expectations for each year of school and to judge and grade all students on how well they achieve those expectations. The difference is that these expectations have been redeveloped and agreed nationally, and there has been some strengthening of accountability arrangements.

However, it is questionable whether higher standards and increased accountability will benefit students who have fallen behind in their learning, reduce levels of disengagement among these students, or decrease Australia's 'long tail' of underachievement. Progress in addressing these challenges almost certainly requires a different set of strategies.

A national key performance indicator (KPI)

One indicator of progress in reducing Australia's long tail of underachievement would be a reduction in the percentage of 15-year-olds not meeting the OECD's baseline proficiency levels as measured by PISA. Figure 1 shows these percentages for reading, mathematical and scientific literacy in 2012. The corresponding percentages for some of the world's highest performing education systems are also shown, indicating the levels that some countries have achieved.

	Reading Literacy	Maths Literacy	Scientific Literacy
Australia	14	20	13
Shanghai	3	4	2
Hong Kong-China	6	9	5
Korea	7	9	6

FIGURE 1 Percentage of 15-year-olds performing below the international baseline proficiency level (2012)

Strategies?

The organisation and delivery of school education have been largely unchanged for decades. Although composite classes are common, students tend to be grouped into year levels by age, and progress automatically with their age peers from one school year to the next. A curriculum is developed for each year of school, students are placed in mixed-ability classes, teachers deliver the curriculum for the year level they are teaching, and students are assessed and graded on how well they perform on that curriculum.

Underpinning this practice is a tacit belief that the same curriculum is appropriate for all, or almost all, students of the same age. This assumption might be appropriate if students of the same age commenced each school year at more or less the same point in their learning. But this is far from the case; the most advanced students commencing any year of school are typically five to six years ahead of the least advanced students. This variability in students' levels of achievement and learning readiness is often underestimated.

As a consequence, the learning needs of some students are not well met. Year-level expectations can be much too ambitious for some less advanced students and not sufficiently ambitious for more advanced students. The challenge for teachers is to meet all students at their points of need with learning opportunities that stretch and extend them. There are several strategies to consider.

Diagnosing where students are in their learning

An alternative to assuming that individuals' levels of readiness and learning needs can be reasonably well inferred from their age or year level is to undertake assessments to establish where students are in their learning. Assessments commonly are undertaken after teaching to determine how well students have learnt what they have been taught. However, to maximise the probability of successful teaching and learning, information is required about where students are in their long-term progress before teaching commences. This information can be collected at varying levels of diagnostic detail. For example, teachers may wish to establish individuals' overall levels of achievement in an area of learning, but also to confirm that they have mastered particular prerequisite skills and/or understandings. The collection of detailed information about where individuals are in their learning prior to commencing teaching is not yet routine practice in many schools.

Personalising teaching and learning

The purpose of diagnosing where students are in their learning before teaching commences is to ensure that learning opportunities are well targeted to individuals' current levels of achievement and readiness. It is now well established that learning is most likely when learners are given activities at an appropriate level of challenge – beyond their comfort zone in what Vygotsky called the 'zone of proximal development' – where learners can succeed, but often only with assistance. Differentiated teaching and personal learning plans are widely used in schools. But these practices sometimes compete with an alternative policy view that the best way to raise standards is to hold all students to the same high expectations, coupled with a belief that this is more 'equitable' than recognising that students have different learning needs. Improved outcomes for less advanced students depend on establishing in some detail the points individuals have reached in their learning and then providing targeted teaching to address specific skill deficits and misunderstandings and to establish stretch targets for further growth. New technologies have the potential to assist in these diagnostic and personalisation processes.

Monitoring learning progress over time

An alternative to simply holding all students in the same year of school to the same year-level expectations and judging and grading them on how well they achieve those expectations is to expect every student to make excellent progress in their learning, regardless of their starting point. In this way, what it means to learn successfully is redefined as the progress (or growth) that learners make. Rather than judging less advanced students as 'poor performers' year after year, the progress these students make is made visible and acknowledged. While every student is expected to achieve high standards eventually, this approach recognises that, because of their less advanced starting points, some students take longer to reach high standards than others. It also recognises that the best way to build students' self-confidence is not to judge and label them as poor learners year after year, but to help them see and appreciate the progress they are making.

Sharing progress with parents and families

School reports typically show how students have performed against year-level expectations and/or the performances of other students. Such information is likely to be of continuing interest to parents. Much less common is information about the progress students have made in their learning over a semester or school year – information that better indicates the amount of learning that has occurred. This information is important because some less advanced students can make good progress during a school year even though they are still below year-level expectations. It is important that parents appreciate this progress rather than concluding from students' low grades that they are poor learners. Failure to recognise and report progress not only provides parents with an incomplete picture of learning, but also can undermine students' understandings of the relationship between effort and success.

The long tail of underachievement is also a long tail of disenchantment with school. Many less advanced students remain or fall further behind with each year of school and become increasingly convinced that they are poor learners and that school is not for them. By the middle years of school, many of these students have become disenchanted and disengaged.

As a nation, we cannot afford to have large numbers of young people marginalised in this way. Part of the solution lies in more flexible ways of organising teaching and learning to better target individuals' current levels of achievement and learning needs. Another part of the solution lies in reconceptualising what it means to learn successfully – defining success and failure not so much in terms of age or year-level expectations but as the progress that individuals make in their learning, regardless of their starting points. In short, the long tail of underachievement will be reduced by expecting and ensuring that every student makes excellent progress every year.

> Editors' note: Following the publication of this essay, results reported from the 2015 cycle of PISA indicated that the percentage of Australian 15-year-olds underperforming against OECD's baseline proficiency levels is increasing when compared to the data in Figure 1: Scientific Literacy 18%; Reading Literacy 18%; and, Maths Literacy 22%.

CHAPTER 6

Getting all children off to a good start

MARCH, 2016, *TEACHER*

Improving quality and equity in our schools to better address the learning needs of the many children who, on entry to school, are at risk of being locked into trajectories of long-term low achievement is one of the biggest challenges we face in school education.

By Year 3, there are wide differences in children's levels of achievement in learning areas such as reading and mathematics. Some children are already well behind year-level expectations and many of these children remain behind throughout their schooling. Many are locked into trajectories of 'underperformance' that often lead to disengagement, poor attendance and early exit from school.

Trajectories of low achievement often begin well before school. Differences by Year 3 tend to be continuations of differences apparent on entry to school when children have widely varying levels of cognitive, language, physical, social and emotional development. Some children are at risk because of developmental delays or special learning needs; some begin school at a disadvantage because of their limited mastery of English or their socioeconomically impoverished living circumstances; and some, including some Indigenous children, experience multiple forms of disadvantage.

According to the Australian Early Development Census (AEDC 2012), 22 per cent of children starting school are 'developmentally vulnerable' in one or more AEDC domains (physical health and wellbeing; social competence; emotional maturity; language and cognitive skills; communication skills and general knowledge). On these figures, Australia has 60 000 developmentally vulnerable children in their first year of formal, full-time school. On average, these children are less likely to make successful transitions to school and are at risk of poorer long-term educational outcomes.

At the same time, children in some population groups are more at risk than others. For example, 43 per cent of Indigenous children are identified as developmentally vulnerable compared with 21 per cent of non-Indigenous children, and 28 per cent of children from low socioeconomic backgrounds are identified as developmentally vulnerable compared with only 8 per cent of children from high socioeconomic backgrounds.

A national key performance indicator (KPI)

National progress in reducing the number of children who begin school at risk of ongoing low school achievement can now be monitored through the AEDC. For example, between 2009 and 2012, the percentage of children judged to be developmentally vulnerable in one or more of the AEDC domains declined from 23.6 to 22.0 per cent.

At a finer level of detail, the AEDC allows the monitoring of national progress in reducing the percentages of 'developmentally vulnerable' children within particular population groups. The percentages for some key groups in 2012 are shown in Figure 2.

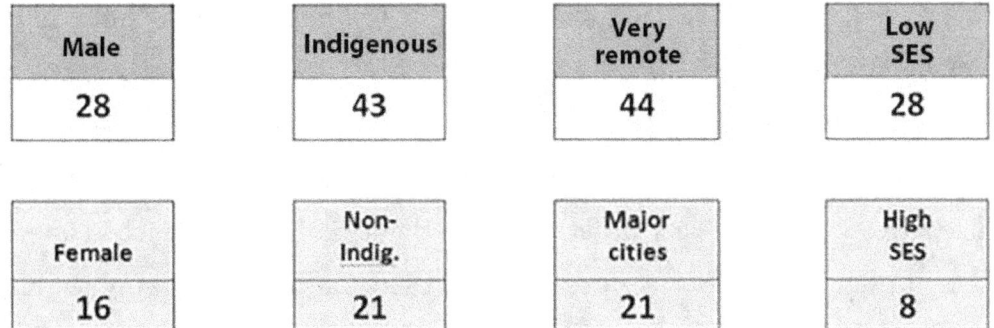

FIGURE 2: AEDC percentages for some key groups (2014)

Strategies?

The challenge of addressing the learning needs of children who begin school well behind the majority of their age group is sometimes described as the problem of children who 'enter school not yet ready to learn'. These children are considered 'unready' for school because of early cognitive and/or non-cognitive 'deficits'. The implication is that more needs to be done by parents, pre-school teachers and other professionals to ensure that all children are 'school ready'.

In reality, children are born ready to learn. They enter school ready to learn. The problem is not that some children enter school not yet ready to learn, but that some children enter school not yet ready to learn what schools are about to teach them or to function effectively in a school environment. Any 'deficit' is a gap between where individual children are in their learning and development and the standardised curriculum and expectations of the first year of school.

Children who lag behind their age group on entry to school often become locked into trajectories of long-term low achievement. Some fall further behind with each year of school and ultimately have poorer long-term outcomes in areas such as employment, teenage pregnancy, mental health and crime (ARACY, 2007).

Although the traditional focus has been on ensuring that all children are ready for school, equally important is ensuring that schools are ready and able to respond to the very different stages that children have reached upon entry to school. In other words, there are twin challenges: to support and promote the progress of all children – and particularly children who lag in their development – in the preschool years; and to ensure that all children make a smooth transition into the first year of school by meeting individuals at their points of need upon entry.

Quality early childhood education and care

Children's learning and development in the preschool years are influenced by a range of factors, including relationships with parents and caregivers, cognitive stimulation, adequate nutrition, health care, and safe supportive environments. Parents' beliefs, attitudes and practices are important to healthy early child development, particularly by providing positive engagement, interaction and stimulation.

Also important is universal access to high-quality, affordable, integrated early childhood education and care, especially in the year before full-time school and for developmentally vulnerable children and children from disadvantaged backgrounds. In Australia, universal access is being facilitated through the National Partnership Agreement on Universal Access to Early Childhood Education and the quality of early childhood provision is being addressed through the National Quality Framework (Early Childhood Australia 2011).

Quality education and care depend on quality teaching (Elliott 2006). In Australia, the Early Years Learning Framework provides broad direction to teaching and learning in the preschool years. The Framework guides curriculum decision making and assists in planning, implementing and evaluating quality in early childhood settings (DEEWR 2009).

Also essential are qualified early childhood educators with well-developed understandings of child development, health and safety issues. Effective pedagogy in the preschool years includes the early detection of developmental delays and the implementation of effective intervention strategies, which in turn depend on the ongoing monitoring of early learning and the tracking of children's social and emotional development.

Smooth transitions into school

An alternative to viewing early childhood education through the lens of 'school readiness' is to recognise that, at any given age, children are at very different points in their learning and development. Rather than focusing on 'deficits' (gaps between children's entry levels and schools' expectations), the focus during the preschool years and also in the early years of school should be on establishing where children are in their long-term learning and development and providing individualised support and learning opportunities to promote further progress.

Seamless transitions from early childhood to school often are complicated by differences in approaches, teaching styles and structures in primary schools and early childhood settings. The greater the gap, the more difficult the transition (UNICEF 2012). Ideally, there would be close collaboration across this transition, with educators meeting and sharing information about learning materials, activities, assessment approaches and outcomes.

Smooth transitions into school also depend on accurate assessments of where children are in their learning and development on entry to school. Baseline data of this kind are especially important for children who enter school with learning and developmental delays. Accurate assessments allow teachers to provide individualised support, including specialist support (e.g. by speech and language therapists) for children who require it. Early childhood educators and parents can make valuable contributions to the collection of information about children's learning and development at the point of transition to school.

Finally, the transition to school is facilitated by planned programs of support and targeted interventions from the moment children start school. The aim should be to ensure a seamless transition by providing optimal learning environments and ongoing close monitoring of progress, especially for children at risk of falling further behind in their learning and development.

Editors' note: Results released through AEDC 2015 indicated that although progress had been made since 2009, around 1 in 5 children were developmentally vulnerable on one or more domain in 2015. Over the period 2009 to 2015, the gap between the proportion of developmentally vulnerable children in the most disadvantaged areas, relative to the least disadvantaged areas, widened across all five domains.

Part 2

IS SCHOOL REFORM WORKING?

Much work has been done over the last decades to identify and describe the qualities of high-performing education systems. However, knowing the qualities of high-performing systems has not in itself provided a roadmap for successful system improvement.

In Australia, despite ongoing reform policies aimed at improving the quality of school education, there is little evidence of improvement. Significant achievement gaps within Australian schools still exist by gender, Indigenous status, socio-economic background and school location and the overall performance of Australian students as measured by international and national assessment programs has either declined or stagnated.

By 15 years of age, 40 000 Australian students do not meet the minimum reading level judged by the OECD to be necessary to participate adequately in life beyond school.

In basic numeracy, the figure is 57 000. Yet, today's 15-year-olds must be innovators and problem-solvers; they must be creators and excellent communicators. They are entitled to an education that equips them with entrepreneurial skills and capabilities that allow them to succeed in the knowledge economy. For Australia to lift student achievement levels, an 'unwavering dedication to the larger educational purpose' is required.

CHAPTER 7

Is school reform working?

DECEMBER, 2014, *POLICY INSIGHTS*, 'IS SCHOOL REFORM WORKING?'
EDITED EXTRACT

Policy settings can make a difference

The observation that students in some countries perform at much higher levels than students in other countries has resulted in international efforts to understand why students in some countries perform so well. These studies show that high national performances tend to be the result of a complex set of factors, including the extent to which particular societies value education and high achievement. For this reason, it is often possible to learn more about effective educational policies by studying countries in which there have been improvements in performance over time. Significant improvements tend to be associated with sustained, long-term policies and deliberate national action to lift performance.

For example, Finland, despite a very recent decline in performance, succeeded in transforming itself from an educationally low-performing country to a high-performing country in about five decades. Underpinning Finland's improved educational performance has been a long-term policy to attract and retain a high quality teacher workforce. Finland raised the bar for entry into teaching and so made teaching a highly selective and highly sought-after profession. Teachers complete a master's degree that includes a research-based dissertation, and there is a strong focus on the development of subject-specific teaching expertise. This focus on teaching excellence is accompanied by policies to educate students in a common, comprehensive school system and to set high expectations for every student's learning.

Countries in which there has been an improvement in student performance over recent decades appear to have placed a particular priority on building teachers' capacities (knowledge and skills) to deliver more effective teaching. Some education systems, including those of Finland and the Shanghai province of China, have trained teachers to undertake systematic research into their own teaching. Through classroom-based research, and with the assistance of diagnostic tools, teachers have been supported to identify and address the learning needs of all students (OECD, 2011).

Another feature of high-performing and rapidly improving school systems is that they have put in place system-wide processes to identify students who are falling behind and to intervene quickly to put students back on track. Finnish teachers are trained to identify students who are slipping behind in their learning and every Finnish school has a teacher who is responsible for working with such students. In East Asian countries, students who are falling behind in their learning stay back after school for remedial teaching. These countries set high expectations for every student's learning.

All students are expected to make excellent learning progress and are considered capable of meeting high standards given time, motivation and appropriate support. Related to this, school systems with early tracking or streaming of students (e.g. into vocational and academic streams), generally have less equitable student outcomes and poorer results overall. Some countries (such as Poland and Germany) have achieved significant recent improvements in student performance in part by delaying the tracking of students (World Bank, 2010).

In summary, deliberate and sustained public policies have made measurable differences to the quality and equity of school education in a number of countries. Factors underpinning improved performance include the development of a high quality teacher workforce; collaboration to promote effective teaching practices; effective instructional leadership of schools; high expectations for every student's learning; and policies to ensure that these practices are distributed across all classrooms in all schools.

Identifying the right drivers

By the turn of the 21st century, the observation had been made in many countries that substantial increases in expenditure on schools had failed to deliver measurable improvements in student performance. This led some economists to conclude that improvements in schools now depended on giving teachers and schools direct incentives to raise student performance.

And some countries have identified another incentive for schools to improve – the risk of losing students to a better performing school.

But there are good reasons to question the effectiveness of accountability regimes and incentive programs as strategies for school improvement. First, the countries that have been pursuing these strategies tend to be the countries that have experienced the greatest declines in student performance over the past decade.

Second, research is raising doubts about the theoretical underpinnings of incentive schemes. Third, although incentives are popular in the world of business, there is growing evidence that financial rewards are not particularly effective there either – except, perhaps, in relatively low-skilled occupations. In professional and creative work, financial rewards are sometimes counterproductive.

In summary, there have been important differences in the primary focus of countries' school reform efforts over the past decade. In some countries, reform efforts tend to have been focused first on building the capacity of school leaders and classroom teachers to deliver high quality teaching and learning, and on ensuring that excellent teaching and leadership are distributed throughout the school system. In other countries, including a number of English-speaking countries, greater reliance has been placed on using systems of accountability and incentives to drive improvement. These two approaches (see Table 1) are not mutually exclusive. However, as Michael Fullan (2011) has observed, some strategies appear to be more effective than others in leading school reform efforts.

Is School Reform Working?

BELIEF	BELIEF
Improvement will occur if schools are given *incentives* to improve (rewards, sanctions, having to compete for students).	Improvement will occur by building the capacity of teachers and school leaders and by ensuring high quality practice throughout the system.
STRATEGIES	**STRATEGIES**
• stronger performance cultures • better measures of outcomes • personal accountability for improvement • performance pay linked to test scores • greater public transparency • financial rewards for school improvement • sanctions for failure to improve • increased competition for students • greater autonomy to compete • more parental choice	• attract more able people into teaching • train approximately the number of teachers required • place a high priority on building teachers' content and pedagogical content knowledge • develop school leaders' capacities to build and lead cultures of continual improvement in teaching and learning • ensure that high-quality teaching and leadership are equitably distributed across all schools

TABLE 1 Two general approaches to school reform.

Editors' note: Following the publication of this essay, results reported from the 2015 cycle of PISA indicated a decline in Australian student performance across Scientific Literacy, Reading Literacy, and Mathematical Literacy (between 2006–2015).

CHAPTER 8

20-year slide in maths and science learning

NOVEMBER, 2016, *TEACHER*

With the release of results from the four-yearly Trends in International Mathematics and Science Study (TIMSS) we now have 20 years of data on mathematics and science levels in Australian schools.

The results are not encouraging. According to the report, *TIMSS 2015: A first look at Australia's results* (ACER 2016) average achievement levels in secondary schools continue to slide in comparison with performances in many other countries.

The gap between Australia, and the world's highest performing country in Year 8 mathematics, Singapore, widened between 1995 and 2015. Only seven per cent of our students now perform at the advanced level in mathematics, compared with 54 per cent of students in Singapore.

We have also been overtaken by a number of countries that we once outperformed, including the United States and England. Australia now performs below 12 other nations, including the Russian Federation, Kazakhstan and Slovenia.

In Year 8 science, the picture is not much better. Levels of science achievement in Australia were unchanged between 1995 and 2015. The gap between Australia and the highest-performing countries widened. Seven per cent of

Australian students now perform at the advanced level in science, compared with 42 per cent of students in Singapore. We are significantly outperformed by the United States and England, as well as by a dozen other countries including the Russian Federation, Kazakhstan and Hungary.

In primary schools the picture is a little more encouraging, with some evidence of improvement in Year 4 mathematics levels over the past 20 years. But for a nation that believes its future relies on increased levels of science, technology, engineering and mathematics (STEM), greater innovation and increased numbers of students studying mathematics and science in the senior secondary school, the latest results are concerning.

Which brings us to the question of what it will take to lift levels of mathematics and science learning in schools.

The answer is not to do more of the same. Reworking the school curriculum, testing students' numeracy levels and maintaining existing approaches to teacher professional development are unlikely to produce world-class improvements.

The answer lies in raising the effectiveness of classroom teaching, which in turn depends on teachers with high levels of mathematics and science knowledge implementing proven teaching strategies.

Currently, the percentage of top-performing school leavers choosing teaching as a career in Australia is in decline. School leavers with high levels of mathematics and science are seeking careers elsewhere. As a result, these school subjects are often taught by less well-prepared teachers. For example, 38 per cent of teachers teaching mathematics in Years 7 to 10 have never studied how to teach mathematics and have not taken mathematics beyond first-year tertiary level. As a nation, we must attract more of our highly able young people into teaching and provide them with training in the teaching of mathematics and science.

Significant improvements also depend on better ways of monitoring where students are in their mathematics and science learning. What do they currently know? What do they not know? What misunderstandings have they developed? Diagnostic information of this kind is crucial for targeting teaching, setting personal learning goals and monitoring individual progress. Teachers, students and parents require clear roadmaps against which they can monitor long-term progress. But quality feedback of this kind is often missing. In its absence, teachers deliver the same year-level curriculum to all students and then grade them on how much they have learnt.

The 20-year slide in maths and science learning is a national challenge that requires a national response. We cannot afford another 20 years of stagnation.

CHAPTER 9

Planning a stronger teacher workforce

MARCH, 2015, *TEACHER*

Ongoing improvements in educational performance in Australian schools depend on continual improvements in the quality of classroom teaching.

Australia faces a number of challenges over the next decade in planning the future teacher workforce. Some of these challenges were helpfully outlined by Dr Paul Weldon in a recent issue of *Policy Insights* (Weldon 2015) and are well worth reiterating here.

At the present time, the supply of teachers in Australia is not well matched to demand. As a nation we do a poorer job than some other countries in ensuring that we prepare an appropriate number of teachers in the areas in which they are most needed.

In some areas we have a significant *undersupply* of teachers. This is true in the area of language teaching, but also is true for the teaching of secondary mathematics, physics and chemistry. We also have an undersupply of appropriately qualified teachers in some regional and remote parts of Australia.

A consequence of undersupply is a growing number of teachers teaching 'out-of-field'. (Teachers are assumed to be notionally qualified if they have studied a subject for at least one semester at second year tertiary level or have trained at tertiary level in teaching methodology in the subject concerned.) It is estimated that 20 per cent of secondary mathematics classes and a similar percentage of physics classes are now taught by teachers who are teaching out-of-field. In geography, 40 per cent of classes involve out-of-field teaching.

On the other hand, Australia has a considerable *oversupply* of generalist primary teachers, with a marked oversupply in some states, including Victoria, South Australia and New South Wales.

There are also many thousands of Australian teachers who are registered to teach but who are not in the teaching workforce. Very little is known about this pool of registered teachers – including the areas in which they were trained or their availability for employment.

Planning for the teacher workforce is complicated by a number of other changes that are occurring in both the demand for, and supply of, future teachers.

First, there will be an increase in the number of teachers required over the next decade.

In the first decade of the 21st century, all Australian states except Queensland and Western Australia saw declines in their populations of primary students. This trend is being reversed in the second decade, with almost all states experiencing significant growth in student numbers. Particularly strong growth is being experienced in New South Wales, Victoria, Queensland and Western Australia.

As an illustration of this turnaround, the primary population in New South Wales declined by 9000 students in the decade to 2010, but in the decade to 2020 is projected to increase by 92 000 students. Secondary schools will see this increase flow through from 2018.

A simple way of estimating the number of new teachers required to service this growth is to assume an average class size of 24 students. By this reckoning, the four most populous states between them will require an additional 1627 classes each year for at least the next ten years.

Second, important changes are occurring within the existing teacher workforce.
An important change over the past three decades has been a decline in the percentage of male teachers in secondary schools. Although the gender mix in primary schools has been fairly stable (with 80 per cent of teachers being female), the percentage of male teachers in secondary schools has declined from a majority (55 per cent) in 1981 to a minority (42 per cent) currently.

At the same time, the teacher workforce is aging, particularly in some areas. In secondary schools, more men than women teach subjects such as physics (75 per cent male), mathematics, chemistry and computing, but the average age of teachers of these subjects is increasing, with 50 per cent of male mathematics teachers and more than 40 per cent of male physics teachers now over fifty years of age.

And a growing number of teachers are choosing to work part-time. The percentage of part-time employment is particularly high among older teachers. Across the age range, 27 per cent of all primary teachers and 20 per cent of all secondary teachers now work part-time.

Third, growing numbers of teacher education students are being drawn from lower ATAR bands.
Important changes also are occurring on the supply side. With the Commonwealth Government no longer controlling the maximum number of funded places in initial teacher education programs, there has been strong recent growth in the numbers of students enrolling in initial teacher education.

Associated with this growth has been an increase in the number of students entering teacher education with relatively low ATARs. There is also evidence that the number of university applicants identifying teaching as their first preference has been quite stable over recent years, suggesting that a growing number of students are entering teaching after failing to obtain a place in their course of first choice.

This trend is of concern because we know that high-performing countries draw their teachers from the top third (and in some cases, the top 10–15 per cent) of school leavers. Students entering teacher education directly from school in Australia tend to be drawn from the middle third of the student distribution. As the Teacher Education Ministerial Advisory Group observed recently, high academic achievement is only one requirement of future teachers. However, high-performing countries tend to require high academic achievement of entering teacher education students, and then select on the basis of skills and personal attributes required for effective teaching. These include interpersonal and communication skills, literacy and numeracy skills and a commitment to teaching as a career.

Planning ahead

Australia currently has an undersupply of teachers in some areas and an oversupply of teachers in others. There are also important changes occurring in the demand for teachers, the nature of the existing teacher workforce, and the cohort of students being prepared to become teachers.

Under these circumstances, it is essential that we have excellent data for workforce planning and a good understanding of developments and trends that will shape the teacher workforce of the future.

The overarching challenges are to ensure that Australia has the numbers of future teachers it requires and is not training too few or too many teachers; that we have teachers in the areas in which they will be required – geographically, by stage of schooling and by subject specialisation, and that we work to ensure Australia's future teaching workforce is drawn from the best and brightest of our school leavers.

CHAPTER 10

Incentives – an ineffective school improvement strategy?

OCTOBER, 2014, *TEACHER*

Performance pay linked to improved test results; financial rewards for school improvement; sanctions for schools that do not meet annual improvement targets; greater competition between schools for students – these are among the 'incentives' that governments and education systems use in an attempt to drive school improvement. But just how effective are incentives as an improvement strategy?

By the turn of the century, the observation had been made in many countries that substantial increases in expenditure on schools had failed to deliver measurable improvements in student performance. International studies showed total national spending on schools, average class sizes, formal teacher qualifications and teachers' years of experience were poor predictors of how well students performed on tests in key areas of the school curriculum.

This led some economists of the time to conclude that 'input-based' policies such as providing more money to schools, reducing class sizes and improving teacher qualifications had 'failed', and that improvements in schools now depended on giving teachers direct incentives to raise student performance:

A simple idea that pervades economics is that incentives have powerful effects. In the case of schools, few incentives relate to the object of interest – student performance (Hanushek 2002).

Over the past 15 years, this simple idea has had a far-reaching influence on the education policies of many countries, especially in the English-speaking world.

Initiatives to provide better incentives for improvement have included the creation of stronger performance cultures in schools, with teachers and school leaders being held personally accountable for improving students' performances. This, in turn, has required better measures of student performance and, in particular, measures that can be compared reliably across classrooms and schools. A number of countries have used test scores to allocate financial rewards for school improvement, performance pay for teachers, and to identify and intervene in schools that fail to meet annual improvement targets.

And some countries have come up with another incentive – the risk of losing students to a better performing school. To promote this incentive, they ensure the public transparency of schools' test results, encourage greater parental choice of schools, and free schools to operate as independent competitors in the marketplace for students.

Examples of such initiatives include the No Child Left Behind legislation in the United States, which required schools to demonstrate that they were making adequate yearly progress and provided escalating negative consequences for schools that were unable to do this; the creation and publication of league tables of 'value-added' measures of school performance in England; proposals to introduce financial rewards for school improvement and performance pay tied to improved test results in Australia; and the encouragement of competition between schools under New Zealand's Tomorrow's Schools program.

But there are good reasons to question the effectiveness of incentives as a school improvement strategy.

First, the countries that have been pursuing this strategy tend to be the countries that have experienced the greatest declines in student performance over the past decade. At ACER's annual research conference in August, I showed how the average reading levels of 15-year-olds changed between 2000 and 2012 in a number of OECD countries (Figure 1):

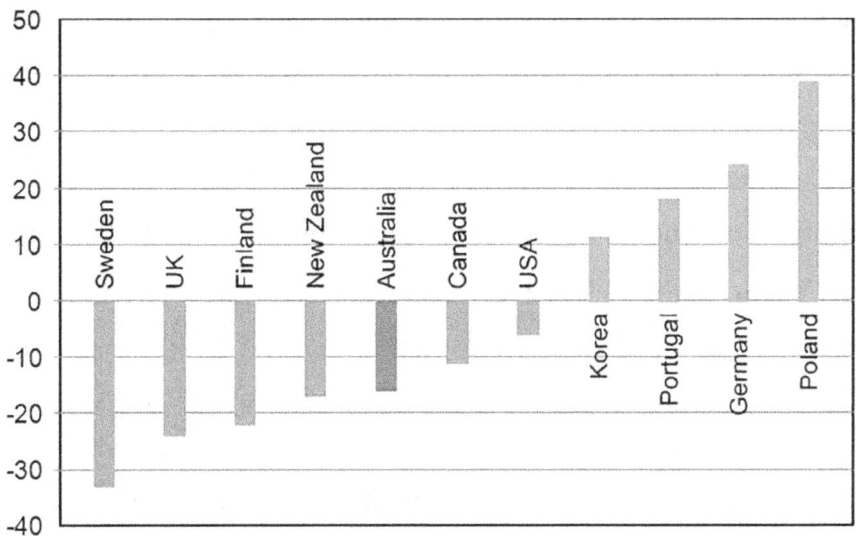

FIGURE 1 Change in performance of average reading levels of 15-year-olds (2000–2012)

Major English-speaking countries saw significant declines in reading levels, and similar declines in mathematics. Although it's not possible to attribute these declines to any specific education policy, it's also hard to conclude that incentive schemes and new school accountability arrangements in these countries have had a positive impact on student performance.

Second, research is raising doubts about the theoretical underpinnings of incentive schemes. A review published by the US National Research Council concluded that the international evidence was 'not encouraging about the ability of incentive programs to reliably produce meaningful increases in student achievement'. Research by RAND Education reached a similar conclusion: 'paying teachers to improve student performance did not lead to increases in student achievement and did not change what teachers did in their classrooms' (Hout & Elliott 2011). And as well as being of questionable effectiveness, incentive schemes often result in unintended and undesirable behaviours on the part of teachers and schools, ranging from the narrowing of the school curriculum, to withholding less able students from testing, to providing inappropriate assistance to students during tests.

Third, although incentives are popular in the world of business, there is growing evidence that financial rewards are not particularly effective there either – except, perhaps, in relatively low-skilled occupations. In professional and creative work, financial rewards are sometimes counterproductive. In fact, there is evidence from psychology studies that paying people for what they would have done anyway can lead to poorer performance. Author Daniel Pink argues that what motivates most people at work is not so much money as the opportunity to self-direct, to master increasingly challenging work, and to pursue a purpose and make a difference in the world.

Whether in the form of pay-for-results, sanctions for not improving, or the threat of losing students to competitors, there is little evidence that current improvement incentives are delivering better student outcomes. To borrow a term from Michael Fullan, incentives appear to be among the many 'wrong drivers' of school improvement.

CHAPTER 11

Focus on the larger purpose of schooling and improvement may follow

FEBRUARY, 2017, *TEACHER*

In his 1946 book, *Man's Search for Meaning*, Viktor Frankl observed that some things, like success and happiness, are achieved not by pursuing them directly, but as 'side-effects' of a dedication to something larger. There may be a lesson here for our efforts at school reform.

In recent years there has been a strong focus on improving the outcomes of schooling – particularly students' literacy and numeracy skills. This is appropriate. For too long we measured only inputs to schooling, such as funding levels and student–teacher ratios. However, despite this recent focus, there is little evidence that outcomes have improved.

One focus has been on closing achievement gaps – particularly gaps based on students' Indigenous and socioeconomic backgrounds. This is appropriate; average literacy and numeracy gaps can be the equivalent of several years of school. However, despite the considerable effort and resources allocated to this priority over recent decades, there is little evidence that gaps have been reduced.

School systems sometimes pursue the closing of gaps directly. They define equity, disadvantage and student needs along socioeconomic lines, allocate resources to schools at least partially on the basis of students' backgrounds;

and design programs and interventions specifically for low socioeconomic and Indigenous students. These systems attempt to close gaps by focusing on gaps directly.

A common assumption is that student groups with different educational outcomes require different educational solutions. The challenge becomes one of establishing 'what works' for Indigenous students or students from low socioeconomic backgrounds. Although large amounts of money have been spent on group-specific solutions of these kinds, achievement gaps remain essentially unchanged.

Of equal concern are the unintended consequences of elevating Indigenous and socioeconomic student classifications in the consciousness of schools. By classifying students in these ways and assigning each school a socioeconomic index, an 'explanation' is proffered for the lower performances of some students and some schools. And it is often a small step from explanation to expectation and then to excuse.

More effective might be an indirect approach to closing gaps. If every student's educational needs were identified and addressed with high quality teaching, high expectations and excellent school facilities and infrastructure – regardless of socioeconomic or Indigenous status – gaps might take care of themselves. Certainly it is hard to see how such a focus could be less effective in closing gaps. An 'equitable' school system would then be one in which every child's needs were adequately diagnosed and addressed and every child made excellent learning progress.

Good measures of progress in improving outcomes and closing gaps are essential. However, success may best be achieved not by pursuing it directly, but as a 'side-effect' of an unwavering dedication to the larger educational purpose.

CHAPTER 12

Achievement gaps – the continuing challenge

JUNE, 2015, *TEACHER*

In society we assign people to groups. Although rules for group membership are always somewhat arbitrary, and group boundaries are fuzzy (even for seemingly straightforward groups such as males and females), the creation of groups simplifies life by allowing us to assume that we know more about a person by knowing the group/s to which they belong.

Of course, there are also downsides. Seeing individuals as group members can make us blind to their individuality. Prejudging can lead to prejudice (words with identical etymological origins). Terrorism and armed conflict depend on the ability to see fellow humans not as individuals, but as members of a group with the presumed characteristics of that group.

In education we assign students to groups. Our reason is the same – we assume that we know more about a student by knowing the group/s to which they belong. When we create groups based on demographic characteristics, we find that some groups have higher average achievement levels than others. For example, urban students generally have higher achievement levels than rural or remote students. Girls tend to outperform boys, particularly in language-rich subjects. Non-Indigenous students outperform Indigenous students, and students from high socioeconomic backgrounds outperform students from low socioeconomic backgrounds. In some cases, achievement gaps are the equivalent of two or more years of school.

One response to this observation has been to assume that the closing of achievement gaps requires *group-based* solutions – for example, special initiatives aimed at boys (or girls), educational solutions for Indigenous students, or government programs targeting students from low socioeconomic backgrounds. However, there is limited evidence that group-based solutions of these kinds have been effective in closing achievement gaps. For example, the literacy and numeracy gaps between Indigenous and non-Indigenous 15-year-olds in Australia were unchanged between 2000 and 2012. The gaps between low and high socioeconomic students also were unchanged. Even where changes have occurred over time (e.g. in the relative performances of males and females, or in Indigenous participation rates), it is not clear that group-based educational solutions rather than broader societal changes have been the cause.

So why are group-based solutions not more effective in closing achievement gaps? Part of the explanation is likely to be that group-based solutions are not relevant to all members of a group. It would be wrong to think that all Indigenous students have similar learning needs. It would be equally wrong to assume that all boys, all girls, or all students from low socioeconomic backgrounds have identifiable but similar learning needs. Initiatives and programs designed for particular groups are not likely to be helpful to all members of those groups.

Another part of the explanation, I suspect, is that effective educational practice is effective regardless of group membership. In other words, we have overestimated the importance of finding and providing group-specific educational solutions. What works for some students tends to work for all students. Highly effective teaching practices tend to benefit all students, regardless of the groups to which they belong. Rather than attempting to develop and implement solutions for defined student groups, a more effective strategy for closing achievement gaps may be to work to ensure that evidence-based best practice is implemented as widely as possible in every school and every classroom.

A related question is whether focusing on demographic groups is not only ineffective but also counterproductive in closing achievement gaps. There is often a small step from observing a correlation – for example, between socioeconomic background and achievement – to treating this observation as an 'explanation'. And from 'explanation', it is another small step to 'expectation' and beyond that to 'excuse'. School principals who have led significant improvements in low socioeconomic areas often report that their first challenge was to confront low expectations based on students' backgrounds. More subtly, concluding that students in a particular school are performing well 'given their socioeconomic backgrounds' or 'given the proportion of Indigenous students in the school' reflects reduced expectations based on group membership.

And there are other ways in which schools set expectations based on group membership. One of these is to prejudge students' learning needs based on their age or year group. Schools continue to be organised on traditional lines with students being assigned to year groups, and teachers delivering the curriculum specified for each year group. However, in learning areas such as mathematics and reading, students in the same year group vary in their achievement levels by as much as five or six years of school. If teachers treat all students in the same year of school as equally ready for the same curriculum, then some lower-achieving students are likely to be left behind and some higher-achieving students are unlikely to be challenged and extended.

Expectations also are set when students are grouped by 'ability' and labels such as 'remedial' and 'gifted' are assigned. The definitions of such groups are inevitably arbitrary; the students in them inevitably have different learning needs; and the educational expectations of included and excluded students are inevitably different. When students are streamed by ability, some students can be locked permanently into lower-level streams that place a ceiling on what they are able to learn and how far they are able to progress. This can exacerbate achievement gaps.

The alternative to seeing students in terms of groups is to see them as individuals. Underpinning this alternative is a belief that, while individuals are at different points in their learning and may be progressing at different rates, every learner is capable of making further progress and eventually achieving high standards if they can be motivated, engaged and provided with appropriate (well-targeted) learning opportunities. Under this approach, starting points for teaching and expectations for learning are established individually rather than inferred from group membership, and excellent ongoing progress is expected of every student regardless of their current level of achievement or the group/s to which they belong.

There is no simple solution to the challenge of closing achievement gaps, but part of the answer may lie in paying less attention to group membership in our educational efforts.

Editors' note: Following the publication of this essay, results reported in the 2017 NAPLAN National Report indicated a persistent gap between the Reading and Numeracy achievement of Indigenous and Non-Indigenous students that has not appreciably changed over time.

Part 3

RECONCEPTUALISING EDUCATIONAL ASSESSMENT

The shift towards evidence-based decision-making in education is driving a fundamental transformation of educational assessment. In this new paradigm, assessment is not about judging and grading; it is about establishing where individuals are in their long-term learning at the time of assessment. Evidence gathered from assessment is used to monitor progress over time and inform and guide future action – whether by teachers in a classroom making decisions about teaching and learning strategies or school leaders or systems managers making decisions about policies and resourcing. Underpinning this paradigm is a belief that every learner is capable of progress if they can be engaged and motivated, and are provided with targeted learning opportunities. What is assessed also matters: domains such as literacy and numeracy are crucial, but assessing general capabilities such as critical thinking, creative thinking, and teamwork, are also increasingly important.

Policies to reform assessment must be part of a broader set of reforms to teaching and learning, including redefining successful learning in terms of the progress or growth that students make over time.

CHAPTER 13

Repurposing assessment

2013, 'REFORMING EDUCATIONAL ASSESSMENT: IMPERATIVES, PRINCIPLES AND CHALLENGES, AUSTRALIAN EDUCATION REVIEW' EXTRACT

A first general challenge arises from the widely held perception that the fundamental purpose of assessment in education is to judge how well students have learnt what they have been taught. Much of the field of assessment, including many assessment concepts and much of the language of assessment, was developed from this perspective.

Over time, attempts have been made to move beyond this traditional conception of assessment. For example, following the introduction of the concepts of formative and summative program evaluation (that is, the evaluation of educational programs in the course of their delivery as well as upon completion), the concepts of formative and summative student assessment were introduced to encourage assessments not only upon completion of a course of instruction, but also during course delivery to inform teaching and learning (Bloom, 1968). In classroom practice, however, formative and summative assessments often differ only in their timing and are undertaken within the same general paradigm of judging how well students have learnt what they have been taught.

Other attempts at assessment reform tend to have divided the field into multiple purposes, philosophies and methods, each with its own protagonists. Rather than reforming the field, these efforts often have produced sub-fields, which usually correspond to the specific methods and approaches being promoted by their proponents as inherently more desirable than others.

This review paper has argued for reconceptualising the essential purpose of assessment. In particular, it has argued that assessments should be seen as having a single general purpose: to establish where learners are in their long-term progress within a domain of learning at the time of assessment. The purpose is not so much to judge as to understand. This unifying principle, which has potential benefits for learners, teachers and other educational decision-makers, can be applied to assessments at all levels of decision-making, from classrooms to cabinet rooms. Generally, the same assessments will be useful both for monitoring the progress that individuals or groups are making over time (that is, assessments of learning) and for identifying starting points for future action (that is, assessments for learning). More detailed classroom diagnostic assessments will sometimes be required to achieve a more complete understanding of where learners are in their learning, for example, by exploring students' specific difficulties and misunderstandings.

Although seemingly simple, this reconceptualisation represents a paradigm shift; one which, it has been argued through this review paper, has significant implications for practice. Most assessment practice is intimately linked to the current model of educational delivery, and any change in assessment practice is likely to impact on educational delivery and vice versa.

Assessment is an integral part of the prevailing model. Its role is to establish how well students have learnt (or in the case of formative assessment, how well they are learning) what teachers have taught. The prevailing view of assessment as judging student success is deeply embedded not only in educational practice, but in society more generally. The grading of student success is ubiquitous – so much so that attempts to reform educational assessment have often accepted summative grading as a given and either assigned it a legitimate place alongside other more 'desirable' and teaching-oriented forms of assessment or argued for particular forms of assessment (e.g. holistic teacher judgements) as the basis for student grades. The simplicity of A to E grades and the (generally erroneous) belief that they convey meaningful information about learning progress have contributed to this situation.

In the 21st century, assessments designed only to judge student success against the performances of other students or against age/grade expectations are no longer adequate. The new purpose of assessment requires practitioners and learners to begin with the belief that every learner is capable of excellent learning progress, whatever their current starting point. If learning is to be judged, then it is more appropriate that judgements are based on the progress that individuals make in their learning than on their ability to demonstrate year level expectations (although there will continue to be some value in monitoring performances against such expectations).

However, assessment reform is likely to be difficult in the absence of broader educational reforms. For example, assessment to establish where students are in their learning is largely pointless if teachers intend to deliver exactly the same content to all students in a class regardless of their current levels of achievement; if the overriding assessment concern is the generation of grades that convey how well students have mastered the curriculum for their year level; or if governments demand graded judgements of student learning. On the other hand, the reform of assessment thinking and practice has the potential to lead and drive improvements in teaching and learning.

Perhaps the most significant challenge in reforming assessment along the lines described in this review paper is that it requires a change in mindset, particularly on the part of stakeholders who consider it 'equitable' to hold all students of the same age to the same absolute achievement standards. Accepting the reality that students in the same year of school are at very different points in their learning and so are likely to benefit from differentiated teaching, different learning targets and different measures of learning success are not a matter of accepting lower expectations for some students' learning. If expectations are couched in terms of student *progress*, then there is no argument or reason why the same high expectations of progress should not be set for all students, regardless of their absolute levels of achievement. Failure to identify an individual's learning needs and attempting instead to infer those needs from group membership (e.g. age or year level) is generally likely to be more 'inequitable' and more detrimental to learning.

From the perspective of teachers, the challenge will hinge on embracing the implications of personalised learning for assessment. Personalisation of learning implies using assessment to establish where individuals are in their learning, setting personal learning goals, providing differentiated learning opportunities, monitoring individual learning progress, and encouraging self-monitoring. As previously noted, personalisation and differentiation are undermined by assessment and reporting practices that fail to recognise individual progress and that judge success or failure only in terms of year level standards or expectations.

Arguments for traditional forms of reporting are sometimes made on the grounds that parents understand grades and percentages. However, in the main, parents do not understand traditional forms of reporting because most grades and percentages lack consistent meanings across teachers, subjects and schools. Regression to these traditional report formats sometimes occurs in response to well-intentioned, but unsuccessful and overly complex, attempts to provide parents with better descriptive information. A long-term educational challenge is to develop alternative reporting formats that provide parents and carers with more usable information about where individual learners are in their ongoing learning, what progress they have made, and what might be done to support further learning.

Education systems and governments are in strong positions to influence perceptions of assessment. On one hand, they can promote a traditional view of teaching as the delivery of a common curriculum to all students in the same year level; assessment as the process of establishing how much of this common curriculum each student has learnt; and reporting as the grading and communication of student success. Or they can promote a view of teaching as the process of identifying and addressing the learning needs of individual learners, assessment as establishing where individuals are in their learning, and reporting as the communication of information about learning progress. Although there is a place for explicit year-level expectations, it is incumbent on education systems and governments to promote practices that do not define success *only* as the achievement of year-level expectations. Such traditional practices run the risk that less advanced learners will be viewed (and will view themselves) as 'poor' learners and that the learning needs of these students will not be identified and addressed. There is a parallel risk that, because year-level expectations are relatively easily met by more advanced learners, the learning needs of these students also will be inadequately identified and they will remain unchallenged. The starting point for assessment and reporting policy must be a belief that all students can and should make excellent learning progress and that the key purpose of assessment is to establish where learners are in their learning in order to promote further learning progress.

Editors' note: This short extract was taken from *Australian Education Review*, 57, which reviews research into assessment, especially in schools; it analyses the pivotal role of assessment in learning and argues for its reconceptualisation by practitioners and policy makers to better support learning. The full text of AER 57 can be found at https://www.acer.org/aer.

CHAPTER 14

Rethinking formative and summative assessment

MAY, 2015, *TEACHER*

It's a popular idea – educational assessments are either 'summative' assessments *of* learning or 'formative' assessments *for* learning. But just how fundamental is this distinction? And is it truly useful?

Establishing where students are in their learning

An alternative is to recognise that the essential purpose of assessment in education is to establish and understand where students are in an aspect of their learning at the time of assessment. This usually means inferring what they know, understand and can do from observations of their performances and work.

The questions of what students know, understand and can do can be asked before, during or after teaching – or without reference to a course of instruction at all.

The questions also can be addressed at differing levels of diagnostic detail. For example, assessments can be used to establish overall levels of student achievement in a subject such as Physics; mastery of particular topics such as energy and mechanics; or the ability to apply Newton's First Law to explain the relationship between force and motion in practical situations. These assessments provide information about increasingly narrow and specific areas of learning, but they differ in degree, not kind. They share the same underlying purpose: to establish and understand where students are in their learning.

Use in planning future action

Information about where students are in their learning can be used to plan future action. This is true whether assessment information is collected as part of a teacher's day-to-day work and used to guide next steps in teaching and learning, or through international programs such as the Programme for International Student Assessment (PISA) and the Trends in International Mathematics and Science Study (TIMSS), and used by education systems to guide future policies and programs.

Information about where students are in their learning clarifies the current situation and assists in identifying starting points for action.

The use of assessment information to guide future action might be described as the 'formative' use of assessment. Because learning is potentially ongoing, most, and perhaps all, assessments in education could be used 'formatively'. The important point is that the term 'formative' best describes a particular *use* of assessment information – not a separate class of assessment instruments or processes.

In the same vein, when assessments are used to guide future action, the ultimate intention is to promote learning. This is true whether assessments are used to guide the work of teachers, students, school leaders or education systems. The use of assessment to guide future action is, ultimately, assessment *for* improved learning outcomes.

Use in evaluating past progress

Information about where students are in their learning also can be used to evaluate *past* progress. Has a student's reading level improved, and by how much? Are average levels of achievement in a school better than they used to be? Has the national performance of a particular subgroup of the student population improved over time? Questions of these kinds are retrospective rather than prospective. They focus on growth or progress over time and might be described as evaluations *of* the learning or improvement that has occurred. The answers to such questions are required to evaluate the effectiveness of teaching strategies, interventions and educational programs, making the assessment *of* learning a vital element of every educator's work.

Assessments to establish the points students have reached in their learning by the end of a course are sometimes described as 'summative'. But again, summative assessments are not a fundamentally different class of assessments. They are simply assessments undertaken at a specific time in students' potentially ongoing learning. Because they generally provide information about the full range of course objectives, and are not designed primarily to identify starting points for further teaching and learning, such assessments typically provide coarse rather than fine diagnostic detail.

Reflection

There is no consistent definition of the terms 'formative' and 'summative' in the assessment literature. Some writers make this distinction in terms of timing alone: summative assessments occur at the end of a course; formative assessments are undertaken while the course is in progress. But the time at which an assessment is made is hardly a basis for a fundamental distinction.

Others define this distinction in terms of intended use: formative to inform future teaching and learning; summative to describe and evaluate past learning. But in other areas of life, we do not measure constructs differently depending on whether we intend to use the results prospectively or retrospectively (although we may seek more detailed information when planning future action).

Still others see the distinction in terms of who does the assessing: formative assessments are undertaken by teachers; summative assessments are externally developed. But some externally developed tests provide detailed diagnostic information to guide classroom teaching and learning, and some teachers construct end-of-course examinations.

And the more recent terms 'assessment *of* learning' and 'assessment *for* learning' suffer from a similar lack of clarity. For example, evaluations of learning progress are essential *for* effective teaching and learning.

Perhaps the time has come to ask whether our attempt to categorise educational assessments as either 'formative' or 'summative' is serving us well. A more unified theory of assessment might begin by observing that the fundamental purpose of assessment in education is to establish and understand the points that students (either as individuals or groups) have reached in their learning at the time of assessment, and that there are then different ways to use this information.

CHAPTER 15

Challenging our most able students

APRIL, 2015, *TEACHER*

The first twelve years of this century saw a steady decline in the reading and mathematics levels of Australian 15-year-olds. This decline was especially marked among our most able students. In 2012 there were fewer Australian 15-year-olds performing at the highest international levels in reading and mathematics than there had been twelve years earlier (Thomson et al. 2013).

This was not the case in many other countries. For example, Korea saw a significant improvement in average mathematics levels during this period. As a result, the gap between Australia and Korea – which had already been quite large – widened by the equivalent of a full year of school over these twelve years.

The proportion of high achievers in Australia is lower than in some other countries from the earliest years of school.

By Year 4, the top 10 per cent of Australian students in mathematics perform at about the same level as the top 40 per cent of students in Singapore, Korea and Hong Kong. By Year 8, this gap has widened, with the top 10 per cent of Australian students performing at about the same level as the top 50 per cent of students in Singapore, Korea and Chinese Taipei (Thomson et al. 2013).

These observations raise questions about Australia's future ability to innovate and compete at the highest international levels in fields such as science, technology, engineering and mathematics. In the knowledge economies of the 21st century, there are likely to be implications for Australia's national productivity and for our capacity to contribute to, and not just consume, advances in these fields.

In a presentation earlier this year to the International Conference on Giftedness and Talent Development, I argued that some of the ways in which we organise and deliver school education in this country may be contributing to the underperformance of our most able students. I gave three examples.

1. Failing to recognise true variability in students' levels of capability and achievement

The vast majority of Australian students progress through school with their age peers. Students are placed in mixed-ability classes and progress more or less automatically from one year of school to the next. This practice is supported by the available research; there is little evidence that either streaming by ability or having students repeat years of school is effective in improving educational outcomes.

However, underpinning this practice is an assumption that students of the same age/year level are at broadly similar levels of achievement. At the start of each school year, all students are assumed to be more or less equally ready for the same year-level curriculum. Each year is treated as a fresh start, and even if information about prior performance is available, it may be seen as largely irrelevant to the task at hand.

In reality, the most advanced students commencing any year of school can be up to six years ahead of the least advanced students in that year level. In reading, for example, the most advanced five per cent of Year 3 students already outperform 20 per cent of Year 9 students (ACARA 2014).

This variability in students' levels of achievement tends to be underestimated in the way schools are organised and school curricula are developed and delivered, and standard assessment processes often fail to illuminate actual student variability. Assessments against year-level expectations generally are not ideal for diagnosing and understanding the learning needs of the least advanced students or for identifying the strengths, talents and learning needs of our most advanced learners.

2. Delivering the same year-level curriculum to all students

Under the assumption that students in the same year of school are at broadly similar levels of achievement, teachers then teach the relevant year-level curriculum, accepting that some students inevitably will learn more of what they teach than others.

However, any attempt to infer a student's learning needs from their age or year level alone risks being significantly wide of the mark. And much teaching does miss the mark. Many less advanced students in our schools are being expected to learn material that they are not yet ready to learn because they lack the necessary foundations, and many of our more advanced students are not being stretched and extended by year-level expectations.

Lant Pritchett at Harvard refers to this as the 'curricular gap' – the gap between where somebody thinks or wishes students were in their learning and students' actual levels of achievement (Pritchett & Beatty 2012). For some students, the year-level curriculum is significantly over-ambitious, leading to frustration, disengagement and eventual dropping out. For others, the curriculum is significantly under-ambitious, leading to boredom, disengagement and failure to maximise potential.

Many years ago, David Ausubel (1968) wrote, 'The most important single factor influencing learning is what the learner already knows. Ascertain this and teach accordingly'. Lev Vygotsky (1978) went one step further – the way to maximise the probability of successful learning is to provide challenges just beyond an individual's comfort zone (in their 'zone of proximal development').

There is anecdotal evidence that, rather than being given challenges in their zones of proximal development, many very able students in our schools are being assigned the same year-level work as the rest of their class. Some teachers appear reluctant to give these students more difficult work or to assign additional, more challenging, activities. Instead, these students are often given 'free time' as a reward for completing set work early. There is also evidence that some teachers feel less confident about their ability to meet the needs of these students – something that may be a particular issue for teachers teaching out of field.

3. Equating high grades with successful learning

The third issue goes to the heart of how we define and measure success at school. Many highly able students are being told that they are performing very well because they are achieving high grades on middling expectations for students of their age.

Students who begin the school year two or three years behind the bulk of their age cohort (and five or six years behind the most advanced students of their age) are already on track to underperform on year-level expectations. Many lag their age cohort and receive low grades year after year. At the other extreme, more advanced students tend to begin each school year well ahead of other students. They commence the year at an advantage and are already on track to perform well on year-level expectations – sometimes with minimal effort.

All of this happens because, almost universally, we define success at school in terms of year-level curricula. But there is evidence, including from

Patrick Griffin's research (2013), that many of our most able students are achieving high grades while making relatively little annual progress in their learning. The lowest rates of year-on-year progress are often made by our most able students.

An alternative way of defining and measuring success at school would be in terms of the progress or growth that students make over the course of a year, regardless of their starting point. Under this approach, excellent progress would be an expectation of every student – even those who began the school year well ahead of their age peers.

A way forward?

There is a deeply entrenched belief among many educators and parents that the role of teachers is to teach the curriculum for the year level; the role of students is to learn that curriculum; and the role of assessment is to judge and grade students on how well they have learnt what teachers have taught. In fact, the requirement that teachers assess and grade all students (using 'A to E' or equivalent) against year-level curriculum expectations is currently built into Commonwealth legislation (*Australian Education Act 2013*).

But just how well does this practice identify and address the learning needs of individual learners, including the most able students in our schools?

An alternative belief system – and one that I believe would better serve the needs of all students – is one in which:

- the curriculum is seen less as a body of content to be taught and learnt by all students in a particular year of school and more as a map of what it means to make progress in an area of learning over an extended period of time

- teaching is seen less as the process of delivering the same curriculum to all students in the same year of school and more as the process of establishing where students are in their learning and providing appropriately targeted teaching and learning opportunities

- learning is seen less as mastering the relevant year-level curriculum and more as making excellent learning progress, regardless of starting point

- learners are seen less as good and poor learners and more as individuals who are at different points in their learning and who are capable of making good further progress if motivated and given appropriate learning opportunities

- assessment is seen less as the process of judging how well students perform against year-level expectations and more as the process of establishing where individuals are in their long-term learning and monitoring the progress they make over time

- reporting is seen less as grading students on how well they have learnt what they have been taught and more as communicating where students are in their learning – that is, identifying and describing what they know, understand and can do at the time of assessment.

Editors' note: Following publication of this essay, results reported in the 2017 NAPLAN National Report indicated that in 2017, the top 5% of Year 3 students outperformed the bottom 20% of Year 9 students in reading.

CHAPTER 16

Monitoring student growth

JULY, 2016, TEACHER

In most areas of learning, growth occurs over extended periods of time. The ability to read with understanding, for example, develops over many years of school. Mathematical understandings and skills also develop over many years. In fact, in most school subjects, greater knowledge, deeper understandings and more sophisticated skills develop throughout the school years. This is also true of general skills and attributes such as problem solving and interpersonal and communication skills, which may develop not only across the school years but throughout life.

For this reason, teachers require a deep understanding of what long-term progress in an area of learning looks like.

Another reason teachers require a deep understanding of the nature of long-term learning progress is that, in any given classroom, students are likely to be at very different points in their learning and development. The most advanced 10 per cent of students in any school grade are typically five to six years ahead of the least advanced 10 per cent of students in that grade. If teachers are to provide all students in a class with learning experiences that will stretch and challenge them, they must be able to differentiate their teaching to meet the needs of students who are at quite different points in their long-term progress.

Much practice in schools does not encourage long-term perspectives on learning. Instead, learning is chunked into school years, semesters, units of work and topics. Defined bodies of curriculum content are delivered within these fixed timeframes, and all students are assessed and graded on how much of the content taught in each timeframe they have successfully mastered. Rather than focusing on where students are in their long-term progress, this approach often treats each new topic (or school year) as a fresh start – a self-contained body of content to be taught, learnt and assessed.

Underpinning this approach is an assumption that students in the same year of school are more or less equally ready for the same learning experiences and challenges. The result is that less advanced students often struggle. Some begin each school year well behind their age peers and unready for the material they are about to be taught. Many receive low grades year after year, not acknowledging the long-term progress they are actually making, and undermining their confidence in the relationship between effort and success. Not surprisingly, many of these students conclude that they are inherently poor learners and eventually disengage from school.

At the same time, more advanced students can remain unchallenged. Because they begin each school year well ahead of their age peers, more advanced students may achieve high grades on year-level expectations with minimal effort. As a result, these students sometimes make relatively little year-on-year progress, develop a sense of entitlement to high grades and also have limited understandings of the relationship between effort and success.

A growth mindset

Because progress in most areas of learning occurs over extended periods of time, it is important to be able to track the long-term progress that students make. This requires a shift in mindset. Rather than judging and grading all students on how well they have learnt what they have just been taught, assessment becomes a process of establishing and understanding where individuals are in their long-term progress. This means identifying the points they have reached – usually what they know, understand and can do at the time of assessment – and monitoring the progress they make over time.

A growth mindset in assessment includes a belief that, regardless of where students are in their learning at any given time, every student is capable of making further progress. Although students of the same age may be at very different points in their learning and may be progressing at different rates, every student is considered capable of successful progress if they are engaged, motivated to make the necessary effort and given appropriate (that is, well-targeted) learning challenges and opportunities. Excellent progress becomes an expectation of every student.

Mapping a learning domain

A prerequisite for monitoring long-term learning progress and meeting individual learners at their points of need is a picture of what long-term progress in a learning domain looks like – in other words, a 'map' of the learning domain that can be used to establish where students are in their learning and against which progress can be tracked.

An essential feature of a map is that it describes what it means to learn, develop, grow or improve. In most areas of learning, progress occurs as students acquire more advanced knowledge, deeper understandings and more sophisticated skills. A map describes and gives examples of increasing levels of knowledge, understanding and skill. Importantly, a map of this kind

MONITORING STUDENT GROWTH

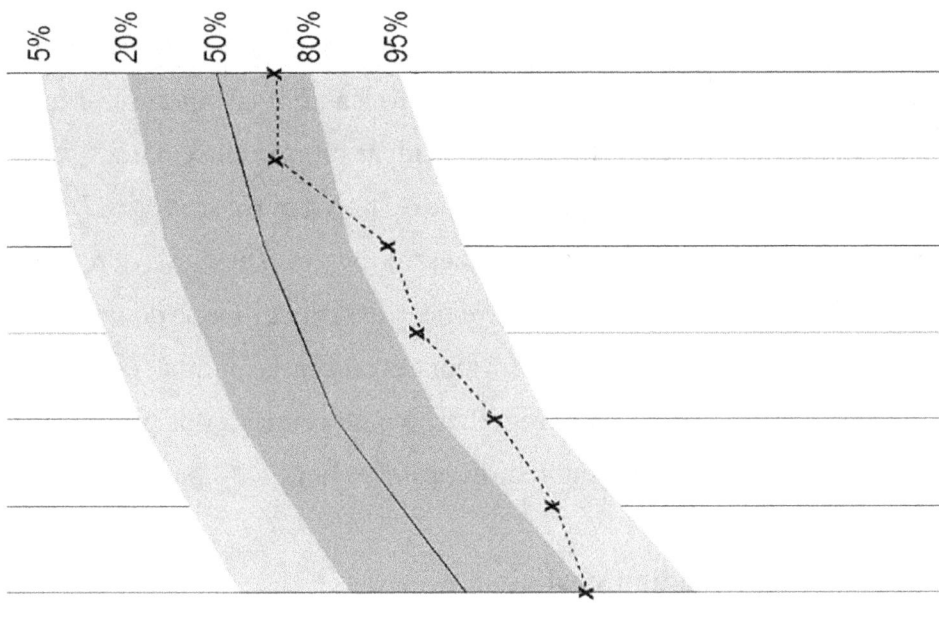

Students at the top of this band can successfully interrogate complex texts in many different ways. They show accuracy and precision in making fine distinctions in the meaning of words, locate concepts that are deeply embedded in strongly competing information, recognise subtle distinctions between ideas, identify implicit arguments and make sophisticated critical evaluations of texts.

Students at the top of this band understand many aspects of complex texts including detailed arguments, dense literary texts with unfamiliar styles and technical texts with unusual diagrams. They interpret detailed reasoning, recognise diverse relationships between ideas and deal with much competing information. They recognise the use of some subtle authorial devices.

Students at the top of this band demonstrate a wide variety of comprehension skills. They can unpack ideas in complex sentences, compare multiple sections of texts and link unfamiliar technical information to a diagram. They make comparisons of tone and style, distinguish opinions from actions, recognise the implications of arguments and extrapolate from given points in texts with substantial complexities, such as sustained metaphors, or succinct texts with significant implied meaning. The complexity of the text, the student's vocabulary and the difficulty of the tasks combine to determine the overall difficulty in comprehending the text.

Students at the top of this band demonstrate a wide variety of comprehension skills including reading closely to make careful distinctions and identifying subtle, scattered clues to support an inference in texts with a key, complex expert such as unusual diagrams, an extended metaphor, some difficult vocabulary or some long, dense sentences. They can link across sections of the text to make a variety of comparisons, identify subtle, scattered clues to support an inference, reflect on the voice or style and use visualisation to support their interpretations.

Students at the top of this band demonstrate a variety of simple comprehension skills where the relevant information is reasonably easy to identify dealing with some competing information and tracking references. They can read and understand a variety of common text types that include an element of complexity such as an unusual voice, a subtle implication or a non-linear timeline.

Students at the top of this band demonstrate a variety of simple comprehension skills such as linking adjacent sections of a text, ordering brief sequences of events, making inferences and reflecting on prominent, familiar features of the text. They can manage low-level competing information. They read and understand a range of familiar, common text types that may include slight complexities such as several clearly implied ideas.

Students at the top of this band demonstrate a variety of simple comprehension skills that mainly concern prominent information in straightforward texts with familiar ideas and structures, some sentence complexity and a few less familiar words. They can directly match words in longer and more complex texts to retrieve adjacent information. They are unlikely to interpret information that is unexpected or in complex sentences or be able to use the context to interpret the meaning of words they don't know.

Students at the top of this band can read and understand prominent ideas and make some details in short, simple explicit texts with a small range of familiar words. They begin to make synonymous matches.

Students at the top of this band can read and understand prominent ideas and make obvious connections in simple unillustrated texts with a few highly familiar words as well as longer texts with supportive illustrations. They mainly use direct word matches to retrieve information. They demonstrate a greater understanding of the text when they can give verbal responses to oral questions.

Students at the top of this band can read and understand some simple, text-based, explicit meaning in texts with highly supportive illustrations that they read themselves. They demonstrate a greater understanding of the text when they can give verbal responses to oral questions.

FIGURE 1 Map of increasing reading proficiency

87

describes progress across a number of years of learning. It is more than a specification of what students are expected to learn; it is a picture of how learning occurs in practice, informed by student performance data.

Levels of increasing reading proficiency are shown in Figure 1, p. 87, with the lowest level at the bottom and the highest at the top. The kinds of reading skills typically observed at each level have been described. These descriptions are based on analyses of students' performances on a large number of reading comprehension tasks. Considered together, the described levels provide the beginnings of a 'map' of growing reading proficiency.

Map of increasing reading proficiency

The shaded regions to the right of the map in Figure 1 show how reading proficiency is distributed and develops from Year 3 to Year 9 in Australia. The lower boundary is the reading level achieved by 95 per cent of students in each year group; the upper boundary is the level achieved by the top five per cent of students in each year group. When students are assessed regularly with the Progressive Achievement (PAT) assessments, it is possible to plot the reading trajectories of individual students against this picture of typical reading development. The dotted line illustrates how one student's reading trajectory might be plotted.

The advantages of a well-mapped learning domain – accompanied by quality assessment processes for establishing where students are in their progress within the domain – include the possibility of teachers, parents and students developing shared understandings of:

- the points individuals have reached in their learning at the time of assessment

- the knowledge, skills and understandings typically associated with those levels of attainment (by referring to the described proficiency levels)

- the kinds of teaching and learning likely to be beneficial in promoting further progress

- the progress (or growth) individuals make across the years of school.

Monitoring growth in this way depends on a growth mindset – a willingness to think in terms of long-term progress and to believe that every learner is capable of further growth, regardless of their current level of attainment.

CHAPTER 17

Towards a growth mindset in assessment

OCTOBER, 2013, *OCCASIONAL ESSAYS,*
'TOWARDS A GROWTH MINDSET IN ASSESSMENT'
EDITED EXTRACT

The approaches we take to assessing learning, the kinds of tasks we assign and the way we report success or failure at school send powerful messages to students not only about their own learning, but also about the nature of learning itself. Assessment and reporting processes shape student, parent and community beliefs about learning – sometimes in unintended ways.

This essay describes three general approaches to evaluating and providing feedback on the outcomes of learning. Each approach is based on a particular way of thinking about what it means to learn successfully, and each has implications for how students view themselves as learners and how they understand the relationship between effort and success.

Assessing growth over time

The third approach is focused on establishing the points that individuals have reached in their learning, setting personal stretch targets for further learning, and monitoring the progress that individuals make over time. Underpinning this approach is a belief that, at any given time, every student is at some point in his or her learning and is capable of further progress if they can be engaged, motivated and provided with relevant learning opportunities. Rather than expecting all students of the same age to be at the same point in their learning at the same time, this approach expects every student to make excellent learning progress over the course of a school year, regardless of their starting point. In other words, this third approach sets high expectations for every student's growth.

Carol Dweck refers to this way of thinking as a growth mindset:

> When [teachers and students] change to a growth mindset, they change from a judge- and-be-judged framework to a learn-and- help-learn framework. Their commitment is to growth, and growth takes plenty of time, effort and mutual support. (Dweck 2006)

When students' performances are assessed from the perspective of a growth mindset, the focus is not so much on 'judging' as on understanding where individuals are in their learning at the time of assessment. What knowledge, skills and understandings do they currently demonstrate, regardless of how other students are performing or what the intentions may be for students of this age or year level? To answer this question it may be necessary to investigate and diagnose in some detail the difficulties that individuals are experiencing or the misunderstandings that they have developed.

Assessment information of this kind provides starting points for teaching and learning. It enables learning activities to be selected and designed to maximise the likelihood of successful further learning. It also assists teachers and students to set targets for learning. Rather than being based on common year-level expectations, these learning targets are personalised; they set realistic stretch challenges for individual learners.

When assessments provide information about where students are in their learning at the time of assessment, they also provide a basis for monitoring individual progress over time. Assessments of progress are an alternative to judging success only in terms of year-level standards. Under a growth mindset, success is defined in terms of the progress each student makes, or the 'distance travelled'.

Importantly, the adoption of a growth mindset does not represent a lowering of expectations. On the contrary, it sets high expectations of every learner, including more advanced students who sometimes are not challenged or stretched and hardly improve at all. Under a growth mindset, 'failure' is defined not in terms of year-level expectations, but as inadequate learning progress.

The adoption of a growth mindset also invites a change in thinking from a belief that there are 'good learners' who meet year-level expectations year after year, and 'poor learners' who perform below standard year after year, to a belief that, although students may be at different points in their learning and may be progressing at different rates, all are capable of good learning progress.

And, when learning is evaluated in terms of the progress that individuals make, the relationship between effort and success is clarified. Students' self-confidence is built, not through success on easy tasks, but when they are able to see the progress they are making, when they appreciate how the quality of their work has improved, and when they succeed on challenging tasks that once were beyond them.

Many existing learning frameworks provide a basis for assessing student growth. School curricula that define clear progressions of learning across the years of school make explicit what long-term growth in a domain looks like, and so provide a basis for establishing individuals' current levels of attainment and for monitoring growth over time. So do a range of empirically-based 'proficiency scales' and 'developmental continua' (Masters 2013).

No small challenge

This essay has argued for defining, assessing and reporting school learning in terms of the progress that individuals make. However, this is no small challenge. Success at school usually is assessed not in terms of the progress that individuals make (e.g. over the course of a school year), but by judging and grading performances against age or year-level expectations. Although letter grades are a relatively recent phenomenon – they appeared for the first time in some North American higher education institutions in the late 19th century and were widely used in schools only in the 20th century – they have come to define what it means to learn successfully at school. Reform depends first on a change in mindset.

Added to this is the challenge of developing credible and easily understood alternatives to current reporting practices. The kinds of reports called for in this essay would provide information about: (1) where students are in their learning at the time of assessment (e.g. what they currently know, understand and can do); and (2) how much progress they have made over some specified time (e.g. a school year, a semester). Good reporting alternatives of this kind generally do not exist. In their absence, the practice of reporting success in terms of year-level expectations is often justified on the grounds that parents wish to know how students are performing in relation to others of the same age. However, this may be less true if parents also had good information about where exactly students are in their learning and what progress they are making over time.

Changing mindsets and developing assessment and reporting tools to support such change are long-term educational agenda. They almost certainly require a transition phase in which processes based on differing mindsets operate in tandem. A starting point is a wider appreciation of the ways in which efforts to provide 'success' experiences and to evaluate learning in terms of common year-level 'standards' fail to engage and challenge some students and encourage fixed rather than 'growth' mindsets in our schools.

Editors' note: In the full-length essay, 'Towards a growth mindset in assessment', Masters draws on Carol Dweck's theory of mindset, arguing that standards-based models of assessment result in students either being categorised as 'good learners' or 'poor learners', and that these categorisations encourage a 'fixed' mindset within students. The full text can be found at https://research.acer.edu.au/rd_school/11/.

CHAPTER 18

The power of expectation

JULY, 2011, *OCCASIONAL ESSAYS*

EXTRACT

Nobody rises to low expectations. Calvin Lloyd

Success in most fields of endeavour depends on an ability to visualise success. It has long been known that elite athletes mentally rehearse each performance prior to its execution. Advances in neuroscience show why this may be so important: the neurological processes involved in visualising a performance are almost identical to those involved in the performance itself. Indeed, simply watching somebody else perform activates 'mirror' neurons in the observer paralleling neuronal activity in the performer (Rizzolatti & Fabbri-Destro 2010). The ability to visualise success and an accompanying belief that success is possible appear to be prerequisites for most forms of human achievement.

It also is clear that the development of self-efficacy is strongly influenced by the attitudes and beliefs of others. In schools, high achievement tends to be correlated with high parental and cultural expectations. Parents, in particular, are powerful inculcators of values and aspirations. Highly influential teachers also are commonly described as individuals who communicate a 'belief' in their students and who build self-confidence through high expectations.

However, just as some students live up to high expectations, so others live down to the low expectations held for them. In education, low expectations are the equivalent of bone pointing; all too often they become self-fulfilling prophecies.

Not surprisingly, students develop differing beliefs about their own abilities to learn. Some students appear to view ability as 'fixed' and something over which they have little control. Students who believe they have low fixed abilities tend to believe that effort will make no difference. Those who believe they have high abilities often underestimate the importance of effort. On the other hand, students with an 'incremental' view of ability have a deep belief that success is related to effort. Rather than interpreting past failures as indicators of a lack of ability, these students are more likely to explain failure in terms of a lack of effort (Dweck 2000). Interestingly, research has identified cultural differences in these beliefs. East Asian students tend to have more incremental views of their abilities than students of European origin (Dweck 2000).

Given its importance to ongoing learning and achievement, few outcomes of schooling are more important than the development of a belief in one's own capacity to learn.

Editors' note: This extract is taken from 'The power of expectation' in which Masters emphasises that the visualisation of success and the belief that success is possible are prerequisites to achievement. The full text can be found at https://www.acer.org/occasional-essays/the-power-of-expectation.

CHAPTER 19

Learning assessments – designing the future

FEBRUARY, 2015, *TEACHER*

Processes for assessing student learning are undergoing fundamental transformation.

Michael Barber and Peter Hill (2014) in their recent paper write of a coming 'renaissance' in educational assessment. Many of the forces for change that Barber and Hill identify are also described in my 2013 paper *Reforming educational assessment: imperatives, principles and challenges*.

So what are these forces for change, and how will they shape the future of assessment?

Three developments underpin the transformation now underway. First, fundamental changes are occurring in how we conceptualise and approach the assessment of student learning. Second, there is growing international interest in, and demand for, the assessment of a broader range of skills and attributes than those addressed in most current assessment efforts. Third, advances in technology are opening the door to new ways of gathering information about student learning, including through records of real-time interactions in online learning environments.

In ACER's Centre for Assessment Reform and Innovation, we refer to these three developments as new thinking, new metrics and new technologies of assessment.

New thinking

It has become common in education to refer to the multiple 'purposes' of assessment. But a conceptual breakthrough is made by recognising that there is only one fundamental purpose of assessment in education. That purpose is *to establish and understand where learners are in an aspect of their learning at the time of assessment.*

The question of where learners are in their learning can be addressed for individuals and also for groups. It can be addressed at different levels of precision and in varying degrees of diagnostic detail. It is an essential question for classroom teachers, but is also crucial for education policy makers and system managers.

Information about where students are in their learning is necessary for identifying appropriate starting points for action. Teachers require information about starting points to target teaching on individuals' levels of readiness and learning needs and to set appropriate stretch goals for further learning. But decision makers at all levels – from students and parents to school leaders to system managers and governments – require dependable information about current levels of achievement to guide future action.

Information about where students are in their learning also is essential for monitoring learning progress over time. Success in learning is best defined and measured as the progress (or growth) that students make. Information about progress is required to evaluate the effectiveness of teaching strategies, but is equally crucial for evaluating initiatives to raise national achievement levels and close achievement gaps.

Under this way of thinking, the focus of assessment is on understanding the current situation and then using this understanding to guide future action, monitor progress, and evaluate the effectiveness of interventions. It has much in common with the use of assessment in other professions such as medicine and psychology, where the purpose is not so much to judge as to understand.

The alternative is to use assessment results only to judge and grade. This use of assessment is consistent with the view that the role of teachers is to teach, the role of students is to learn, and the role of assessment is to establish how well students have learnt what they have been taught – and to grade them accordingly. When used in this way, learning assessments are often viewed as straightforward and unproblematic.

New metrics

Around the world, school curricula are giving greater emphasis to skills and attributes believed to be important for life and work in the 21st century. These skills and attributes – sometimes referred to as general capabilities, cross-curricular skills or 21st century skills – include literacy and numeracy, problem solving, oral communication, critical and creative thinking, the ability to work in teams, self-management, and intercultural understanding. The growing use of new technologies is requiring new ICT capabilities, including new skills in reading, communicating, online searching, and problem solving.

Greater priority also is being given to students' deep understandings of school subjects and their ability to apply those understandings to practical, real-world problems. This is sometimes referred to as a 'literacy' perspective. For example, 'scientific literacy' is defined as the ability to apply scientific knowledge and an understanding of scientific concepts and principles to everyday situations and problems.

These developments introduce a number of assessment challenges. First, considerable work is required to clarify newly prioritised aspects of learning such as creative thinking and collaborative problem solving. A related question is whether skills and attributes of these kinds can be treated as general competencies or whether they have meaning only in the context of specific school subjects. And other questions arise about the focus of assessment. For example, in assessing 'teamwork', is the focus on how well an individual works in and contributes to a team, or should the work of the entire team be the focus of assessment?

Second, constructs of these kinds usually require assessment methods very different from those used to assess mastery of curriculum content. Many require direct observations of learners' performances in complex situations, possibly working collaboratively to solve real problems, to apply what they have learnt, think critically, create new solutions, communicate with others, and make effective use of technology.

Third, because general capabilities such as critical thinking, self-management and intercultural understanding develop throughout the years of school, assessment processes must be capable of monitoring students' long-term development. The same is true of deep understandings of concepts and principles, which often develop only over extended periods of time. The implications are that assessment processes must be underpinned by pictures of what long-term improvements in these skills, attributes and understandings look like – that is, by learning 'metrics' for monitoring progress across multiple years of school.

New technologies

Advances in technology have the potential to transform assessment practice through more personalised, more interactive and more intelligent forms of evidence gathering, as well as by providing more immediate, high-quality feedback about learning processes.

Technology is providing enhanced learning and assessment environments. For example, in school science classes, students are manipulating variables such as forces, angles, distances and time and observing the effects of these changes in virtual environments that are sometimes difficult or impossible to create in normal classrooms. They are conducting on-screen experiments and recording and analysing their observations and measurements electronically. Such technology-enhanced environments provide unique opportunities to collect evidence about students' knowledge and understandings, including by tracking the processes they follow in attempting to solve problems.

Technology also is enabling more personalised forms of assessment in which tasks are matched automatically to the real-time performances of individual students. By selecting tasks at an appropriate level of difficulty, 'computer adaptive' assessments of this kind provide more relevant assessment experiences and superior information about where individuals are in their learning. Students also can be given greater control over assessment processes; for example, by choosing where and when they wish to be assessed.

Finally, it is possible to build into digital assessments expert knowledge about common student errors and misunderstandings and to use this knowledge to automate diagnosis and guidance. For example, if a student when prompted to add the fractions $2/3$ and $1/4$, gives the answer $3/7$, an automatic hypothesis could be generated about the process the student followed. This hypothesis could be tested by assigning other fractions addition tasks. The results of such exploration could be flagged for the teacher's attention and/or lead to electronic tutoring in adding fractions.

A professional challenge

These developments, together with scientific advances in our understanding of learning itself, can be expected to transform school assessment processes over the next decade.

Part 4

SCHOOLS AS LEARNING ORGANISATIONS

In our rapidly changing society, education systems have been slow to keep pace with change. Many schools remain much the same today as they were a generation ago. Many teachers are yet to adopt the necessary pedagogies and practices required to meet the diverse needs of 21st century learners.

It is time for reform. The ultimate goal of school improvement is to improve outcomes for all students. Our schools must become learning organisations, where a willingness to learn from evidence, to acknowledge not just success, but also failure, and to learn from practice are shared and embraced throughout the school and the broader community.

Schools as learning organisations are collaborative learning environments, with a continuous improvement culture. To attain educational excellence, to address the ongoing inequity across Australian schools, to prepare all young Australians for the knowledge economy, deep change and the reconceptualising of learning environments is required.

CHAPTER 20

Schools as learning organisations

JUNE, 2016, *TEACHER*

School improvement occurs when schools learn how to improve. More specifically, improvement occurs when schools identify and implement changes to practice that result in improved student outcomes.

An essential requirement for learning how to improve as a school is a belief that improvement is possible. This requirement might be described as a 'growth mindset for schools' – a belief that, no matter how well or poorly a school is performing, improvements in current practices (and thus student outcomes) are always possible. The opposite – a 'fixed mindset' – is a belief that external factors such as students' socioeconomic backgrounds, available school resources or current levels of achievement limit what is possible and make further improvement unlikely.

School improvement is most likely when an entire school has a shared improvement agenda and is committed to learning how to improve. In a learning organisation, members commit to learning together and to sharing what is learned throughout the organisation. In schools, this means collaborating to find ways to improve current school and classroom practices.

Much learning in schools occurs in informal and unplanned ways as teachers and school leaders introduce new initiatives, try new approaches and learn from experience. But organisational learning can be accelerated when schools adopt a systematic approach to learning how to improve.

In my paper *Schools as Learning Organisations* (Masters 2016), I describe a collaborative methodology for investigating ways to improve current school practices. It's not rocket science. It's a plan for improvement that involves five steps, the central step being the design and implementation of specific improvement strategies.

Current school improvement plans often do little more than identify desired improvements (e.g. improve Year 5 literacy and numeracy results, reduce behaviour problems or improve Year 12 results) or identify actions that a school intends to take (e.g. employ a literacy specialist, introduce a new health and wellbeing program, or partner with a local industry). The kind of plan I describe is a systematic plan for designing, implementing, evaluating and learning from individual improvement efforts. It's a plan for learning as a school.

The five steps in the methodology can be thought of as elements of a potentially ongoing improvement cycle, as shown in Figure 1:

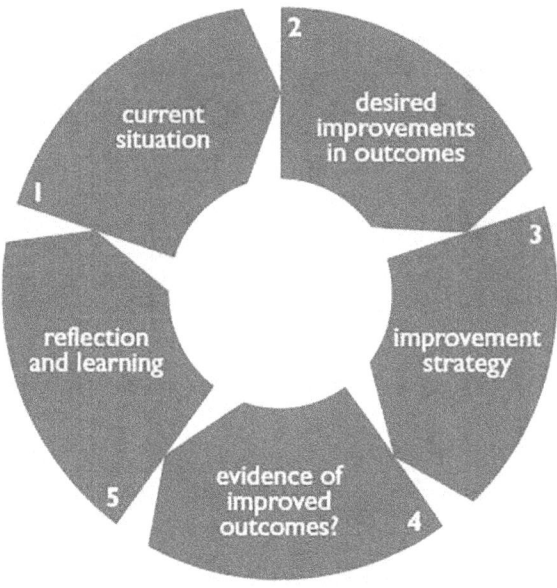

FIGURE 1 School improvement cycle: the five steps methodology

1. Knowing where you are as a school (current situation)

A plan to improve depends first on a good understanding of existing school practices and student outcomes, particularly current levels of student attainment. These are the starting points for any improvement effort and the baselines against which a school's improvement efforts are evaluated.

Information about current student outcomes and prevailing school practices must be collected systematically and reliably. It is not possible to draw meaningful conclusions about improvements in outcomes or practices if this initial information is unreliable. Data need to be collected objectively and dispassionately, and reflect the realities of the school's current performance – not somebody's intentions or beliefs about what is happening in the school.

2. Specifying desired outcome improvements

A school improvement plan specifies what improvements in outcomes a school wishes to see. Desired improvements may include, but are not limited to, improvements in student achievement, school attendance, post-school destinations, and student attitudes and engagement. This step usually involves answering questions such as:

- Which student outcomes do we most want to improve?

- What level of improvement should we be aiming for?

- On what timeline?

A school improvement plan recognises the need to prioritise, set realistic expectations, and provide the time required for meaningful and sustainable improvement.

3. Designing and implementing an improvement strategy

Once a school has decided the outcomes it wishes to improve, the next step is to decide how those improvements will be achieved, that is, the strategy or strategies the school intends to implement. The *National School Improvement Tool* (Masters 2012) can be helpful in designing improvement strategies.

In general, better student outcomes are achieved through more effective, evidence-based school and classroom practices. A school improvement plan makes explicit the changes in practice a school intends to make. The plan also identifies what will be required to implement the strategy, for example, changes in culture, staff professional development, staff redeployment or the physical resources required for effective implementation.

4. Measuring and monitoring improvements in outcomes

The fourth step is to decide how improvements in outcomes will be measured and confirmed. Questions include:

- Was there a measurable improvement in the outcomes the school was trying to improve?

- What is the evidence?

- How confident can we be that an apparent improvement was real?

Conclusions about improvements require measures that can be compared over time and possibly across different instruments. Changes must also be large enough to indicate meaningful improvements rather than chance fluctuations. And conclusions about improvements can be made with more confidence when there is evidence of a trend in outcome measures over an extended period.

5. Reflecting on what has been learned

Finally, a school improvement plan should include a plan for reflecting on, and learning from, the improvement effort. The goal should be to review the implementation of the improvement strategy and evaluate its impact on the targeted outcomes. Questions include:

- What, if any, difficulties were encountered in implementing the planned improvement strategy?

- Did school practices change as intended?

- Was the strategy itself responsible for observed improvements in student outcomes?

- How sustainable are the improvements?

- If there was no improvement, what lessons can be learned?

Answers to such questions guide the school's future improvement efforts. The implementation of this five-step methodology provides a systematic way of exploring the impact of changed school and classroom practices on improved student outcomes. As such, it contributes to a continuous improvement culture underpinned by:

- a belief that continual improvement is possible

- a shared commitment to an explicit improvement agenda

- an understanding that improvement depends on learning how to improve as a school community

- an understanding that professional learning is accelerated by the disciplined study of individual improvement efforts.

'This is not about 'revolutionary' change, but rather about 'evolutionary' change – starting from where you are, experimenting, adapting and learning by doing – with all changes based on evaluated evidence (Collarbone 2015).

CHAPTER 21

National School Improvement Tool

**2012, *NATIONAL SCHOOL IMPROVEMENT TOOL*
EDITED EXTRACT**

Research is revealing the powerful impact that school leadership teams can have in improving the quality of teaching and learning. Effective leaders create cultures of high expectations, provide clarity about what teachers are to teach and students are to learn, establish strong professional learning communities and lead ongoing efforts to improve teaching practices.

The *National School Improvement Tool* (Masters 2012) was endorsed by the Standing Council on School Education and Early Childhood (SCSEEC) at its meeting on 7 December 2012 and has been made available to all Australian schools for use in their school improvement planning from 2013.

The *National School Improvement Tool* brings together findings from international research into the practices of highly effective schools and school leaders. The *Tool* assists schools to review and reflect on their efforts to improve the quality of classroom teaching and learning. It supports school-wide conversations – including with parents and families, school governing bodies, local communities and students themselves – about aspects of current practice, areas for improvement and evidence that progress is being made.

The *Tool* does not describe everything that effective schools do, but focuses on those practices that are most directly related to school-wide improvements, and thus outcomes for students. In this sense, the *Tool* can be thought of as a core element of more comprehensive school improvement programs, frameworks and initiatives.

The ultimate goal of school improvement is to improve outcomes for students, including levels of achievement and wellbeing. For this reason, direct measures of student outcomes are essential to all school improvement efforts. However, 'school improvement' fundamentally means improving what a school does. The *Tool* provides evidence about a school's day-to-day work to complement, and possibly shed light on, measures of student outcomes.

The *Tool* consists of nine interrelated 'domains'. Although the *Tool* has been designed to enable a judgement in relation to each domain separately, experience suggests that the most effective way to use the *Tool* is to make observations and gather evidence broadly about a school's practices before focusing on individual domains. Schools may then decide to give priority to particular domains in their improvement efforts.

A key feature of the *Tool* is the set of performance levels, 'Low', 'Medium', 'High' and 'Outstanding'. These levels enable schools to make judgements about where they are on their improvement journeys, to set goals and design strategies for improvement, and to monitor and demonstrate school improvement over time.

Nine interrelated domains

1. An explicit improvement agenda

The school leadership team and/or governing body have established and are driving a strong improvement agenda for the school, grounded in evidence from research and practice and expressed in terms of improvements in measurable student outcomes. Explicit and clear school-wide targets for improvement have been set and communicated to parents and families, teachers and students, with accompanying timelines.

2. Analysis and discussion of data

A high priority is given to the school-wide analysis and discussion of systematically collected data on student outcomes, including academic, attendance and behavioural outcomes, and student wellbeing. Data analyses consider overall school performance as well as the performances of students from identified priority groups; evidence of improvement/regression over time; performances in comparison with similar schools; and, in the case of data from standardised tests, measures of growth across the years of school.

3. A culture that promotes learning

The school is driven by a deep belief that every student is capable of successful learning. A high priority is given to building and maintaining positive and caring relationships between staff, students and parents. There is a strong collegial culture of mutual trust and support among teachers and school leaders, and parents are treated as partners in the promotion of student learning and wellbeing. The school works to maintain a learning environment that is safe, respectful, tolerant, inclusive and that promotes intellectual rigour.

4. Targeted use of school resources

The school applies its resources (staff time, expertise, funds, facilities, materials) in a targeted manner to meet the learning and wellbeing needs of all students. It has school-wide policies, practices and programs in place to assist in identifying and addressing student needs. Flexible structures and processes enable the school to respond appropriately to the needs of individual learners.

5. An expert teaching team

The school has found ways to build a school-wide, professional team of highly able teachers, including teachers who take an active leadership role beyond the classroom. Strong procedures are in place to encourage a school-wide, shared responsibility for student learning and success, and to encourage the development of a culture of continuous professional improvement that includes classroom-based learning, mentoring and coaching arrangements.

6. Systematic curriculum delivery

The school has a coherent, sequenced plan for curriculum delivery that ensures consistent teaching and learning expectations and a clear reference for monitoring learning across the year levels. The plan, within which evidence-based teaching practices are embedded, and to which assessment and reporting procedures are aligned, has been developed with reference to the Australian Curriculum or other approved curriculum and refined collaboratively to provide a shared vision for curriculum practice. This plan is shared with parents and families.

7. Differentiated teaching and learning

The school places a high priority on ensuring that, in their day-to-day teaching, classroom teachers identify and address the learning needs of individual students, including high-achieving students. Teachers are encouraged and supported to monitor closely the progress of individuals, identify learning difficulties and tailor classroom activities to levels of readiness and need.

8. Effective pedagogical practices

The school principal and other school leaders recognise that highly effective teaching is the key to improving student learning throughout the school. They take a strong leadership role, encouraging the use of research-based teaching practices in all classrooms to ensure that every student is engaged, challenged and learning successfully. All teachers understand and use effective teaching methods – including explicit instruction – to maximise student learning.

9. School–community partnerships

The school actively seeks ways to enhance student learning and wellbeing by partnering with parents and families, other education and training institutions, local businesses and community organisations. Parents and families are recognised as integral members of the school community and partners in their children's education. Partnerships are strategically established to address identified student needs and operate by providing access to experiences, support and intellectual and/or physical resources not available within the school. All partners are committed to the common purposes and goals of partnership activities. Procedures are in place to ensure effective communications and to monitor and evaluate the intended impacts of the school's partnerships.

CHAPTER 22

Essential teaching practices – do they exist?

DECEMBER, 2014, *TEACHER*

It is often observed that there is no single best way to teach – that what works for some learners under some conditions does not work for all learners under all conditions. For this reason, it is argued, teachers require a broad repertoire of teaching methods that they can call on as appropriate.

Evaluations of specific teaching approaches (such as Bloom's Mastery Learning or Engelmann's Direct Instruction) suggest that almost all teaching methods can be effective for at least some students if implemented by committed and highly competent teachers.

Nevertheless, reviews of research identify some classroom practices as more highly correlated with improved student outcomes than others (Sammons & Bakkum 2013; Muijs et al. 2014; Rosenshine 2012). Effective practices include: connecting new material to earlier learning; clarifying learning objectives; explicitly teaching and modelling new material; and regularly checking for student understanding. Other practices such as 'formative assessment' and 'feedback' are also sometimes identified as effective, although the meanings of these terms and the ways in which they are implemented tend to vary across research studies.

An interesting question is whether there are general principles of effective teaching, regardless of who is being taught, what they are being taught or the teaching context. I suspect that there are, and that generations of teachers – from master sculptors to piano teachers to sports coaches to parents of very young children – have used these principles naturally in their everyday teaching. But if such principles exist, how well are they reflected in common education policies and practices?

Here are several practices that I would advance as part of the generic 'essence' of effective teaching.

Establishing where learners are in their progress

Effective teaching depends on an understanding of where individuals are in their learning or development. Highly effective teachers, trainers and coaches work to establish and understand the points that individuals have reached – in other words, their current levels of skill, knowledge and understanding. They pay close attention to the errors that individuals are making, the skills they have not yet mastered and the misunderstandings they have developed. This process of establishing and understanding where learners are in their learning also involves connecting with learners as individuals; for example, by developing an appreciation of their personal goals and motivations.

This element of effective teaching has parallels with practice in other professions such as medicine and psychology where, prior to taking action, information is first gathered to establish and understand the presenting situation and to identify the specific needs of individuals. In many professions, data gathering and detailed diagnosis are prerequisites for informed professional practice.

It is not difficult to visualise teaching that does not include such practice. We all experienced teachers who saw their role simply as delivering the relevant course content. Under this form of 'teaching', no effort is made to understand individuals' varying starting points and learning needs. The role of the teacher is merely to deliver the course content; the role of students is to learn that content; and the role of assessment is to establish how much of what has been taught students have successfully learnt. Delivery is to the group, and individuals are assumed to be equally ready for the course content based on their age or stage of education.

Much teaching in schools continues to be of this latter kind, sometimes encouraged by curricula that specify what all students of the same age should be taught and expected to learn, and by assessment and reporting regimes that judge and grade students on how well they have mastered common age or year-level expectations. When teachers see their role as delivering the same curriculum to all students, and the onus for successful learning is placed solely on students themselves, there is little incentive for teachers to go to the trouble of identifying where learners are in their long-term learning progress.

Tailoring teaching to the needs of individual learners

Effective teachers understand instinctively that learning depends on providing individuals with challenges and learning opportunities appropriate to their current levels of attainment. In other words, they know intuitively how to meet learners at their points of need. They know that learning is unlikely when assigned tasks are so easy that they present no challenge or so difficult that they cause learners to give up in despair. Instead they provide carefully designed stretch challenges that are just beyond individuals' comfort zones – in what Vygotsky called the 'zone of proximal development'.

In any given year of school, students' achievement levels vary by the equivalent of five or six years of school, meaning that students of the same age and year level are at very different points in their learning and have very different learning needs. Some students require significant remedial support; others are unlikely to be challenged or extended by year-level curriculum expectations. Effective teachers are sensitive and responsive to this variability in students' levels of educational attainment and progress. They work to ensure that every learner is presented with an appropriate level of challenge, including already high-achieving students.

Again, it is not difficult to visualise the opposite of such practice – undifferentiated teaching that makes no attempt to accommodate the different starting points and learning needs of individuals, delivers the same content to all students, and judges success in terms of the same learning goal (mastery of the body of taught content). Research suggests that differentiation is a challenge for some teachers, especially in secondary schools. It is likely that many less-advanced students in our schools are being given material for which they are not yet ready, and many more-advanced students are being given material that fails to challenge or extend them.

Providing immediate feedback to guide action

Learning of all kinds is facilitated by high quality feedback. Some of the most effective users of feedback are parents of young children who use it to correct, guide and teach. The feedback parents provide is opportunistic, immediate, personalised, action-focused, supportive and ongoing – features that also characterise the feedback of expert sports coaches, trainers and mentors. The feedback that classroom teachers provide is likely to be most helpful to learning when it shares these features.

In contrast to ongoing, opportunistic feedback is feedback that is planned and episodic (e.g. provided only in relation to specific assessment events or assignments). There is usually a delay in feedback of this kind, and when it is provided, details capable of guiding learning often receive less student attention than overall judgements of the quality of their work (e.g. B+). To the extent that feedback is planned, delayed and primarily judgemental, it is generally less useful for guiding student action. The quality of the feedback students receive often declines through the years of school, with younger children being more likely to receive feedback that is opportunistic, immediate and action-focused, and older students more likely to receive feedback that is planned, delayed and judgemental.

Assisting learners to see and appreciate the progress they are making

Effective teachers also understand the importance of assisting learners to see the progress they are making over time. They know that this is one of the best ways to build individuals' beliefs in their ability to learn and improve, and so is important to motivation and effort. Some progress is easily measured (e.g. improvements in an athlete's times), but in other contexts, effective teachers find ways to help learners see how the quality of their work or performance has improved over time and to recognise how they are now able to perform tasks that once were beyond them.

Schools often do a poor job of helping students see and monitor long-term learning progress. Part of the reason is that schooling is delivered in discrete time periods (school years, semesters, courses, units of work). Each new time period tends to be treated as a fresh start, with students being judged and graded on how well they perform in each period separately. One consequence is that limited information is passed from one learning period to the next. For example, there are few long-term pictures of student progress across multiple years of school. A second consequence is that the grades students receive often disguise the progress they are making. For example, a student who receives a 'D' year after year is unable to see their long-term progress and, worse, may conclude that there is something stable about their ability to learn (that is, they are a 'D student').

We now know enough about teaching and learning to know that no single, pre-packaged teaching solution works for all learners in all situations. But it does not follow that there are no general principles of effective teaching. A challenge is to continue to identify the essence of effective teaching, wherever it occurs.

CHAPTER 23

Learning from mistakes

MAY, 2016, TEACHER

In his book *Black Box Thinking*, Matthew Syed argues that some organisations and fields of endeavour are better than others at learning from mistakes.

Syed names healthcare as an area that, historically, has been slow to learn from mistakes. Too often, he argues, healthcare mistakes are stigmatised, doctors are expected to be infallible, and systems are set up to ignore and deny errors rather than to investigate and learn from them. Data are not always collected and analysed in ways that allow learning; poor practices and mistakes go undetected; and, in the English-speaking world alone, tens of thousands of patients die each year as a direct result of medical errors.

On the other hand, Syed argues, the aviation industry has developed an admirable willingness and tenacity to investigate the reasons for failure. It has created systems and cultures that enable the entire industry to learn from individual mistakes.

The title of Syed's book is a reference to the 'black box' flight recorder. He draws a parallel with the way science progresses through a process of self-correction that depends on testing ideas, subjecting them to failure and profession-wide learning.

Syed concludes that learning from mistakes depends on:

- a willingness to learn from failure

- investigative skills and systems to extract and promulgate key lessons from mistakes.

Willingness to learn

A willingness to acknowledge and learn from failure is essential for all progress. Obstacles to acknowledging mistakes include the desire to protect personal reputations and deeply held beliefs. However, when evidence is avoided, hidden or ignored, learning opportunities are lost. This is true at the level of individuals and is equally true at the level of organisations, industries and professions.

Learning from failure is facilitated by a culture that accepts mistakes and welcomes the learning opportunities they provide. The fear of blame undermines the possibility of learning. Openness to learning requires personal and organisational resilience – an ability to acknowledge failure and to treat it as a learning opportunity.

Systems and skills

Learning from failure also depends on systems and skills to investigate, analyse and understand errors. As Syed notes, often this means looking beyond the obvious data to the underlying explanations or causes. Feedback on the reasons for mistakes and failures is essential to learning. But the identification of underpinning explanations usually requires well-honed skills of investigation.

Syed concludes that the paradox of success is that it is built on failure: 'every error, every flaw, every failure, however small, is a marginal gain in disguise'. Evolutionary progress depends on feedback about what is working and what is not. Without such feedback, learning is severely constrained.

How well does education learn from mistakes?

It is interesting to reflect on our attitudes to mistakes and failures in education.

To what extent are we prepared to call a government initiative that produced no measurable improvement a 'mistake'? How often do we identify educational resources and programs as 'failures'? Are we prepared to call the widespread promotion of an ineffective teaching strategy an 'error'? Do we jump too quickly to defend and rationalise our efforts as well-intentioned and perhaps not entirely unsuccessful? And how well do we learn from such missteps?

Of course, education is not the only public policy area in which initiatives are inadequately evaluated, thereby providing little opportunity for learning. Many policy initiatives are based on personal ideologies or beliefs about what should work. Many are implemented on short timelines within the constraints of political cycles and disappear with changes in governments, ministers or senior bureaucrats. But when education policies and initiatives are denied the opportunity to fail (or to succeed), governments, education systems and the profession are denied opportunities to learn.

A willingness to learn not only means allowing time for success or failure, it also means committing to investigating why initiatives have succeeded or failed. Too often in education, policies and programs are introduced with no accompanying plan to evaluate and study their impact. Learning from mistakes requires a learning culture: a commitment to a long-term agenda to learn from evidence; a willingness to evaluate, identify and acknowledge successes and failures; and agreed systems for investigating and learning from practice.

Learning from student mistakes

There are implications, too, for our attitudes to failure in the classroom. If mistakes are essential to learning, to what extent do we design teaching to produce mistakes? Or do we instead stigmatise failure by sending students the message that we do not expect mistakes and that successful learning means not making errors?

One way to minimise mistakes is to assign tasks within students' comfort zones. If tasks are relatively easy, failure is unlikely. But so too is learning. Successful learning is most likely when students are given challenges beyond their comfort zones – challenges that stretch and extend them to the point of making mistakes from which they can learn.

A first requirement then is a willingness to see mistakes not as something to be avoided, but as something to be embraced. This has implications for both teachers and students. Much teaching is focused on creating conditions for student success. But effective teaching often means providing opportunities for students to make mistakes and to learn. Students need to be assisted to welcome new challenges and to view mistakes not as reflections on their ability, but as vital steps in the learning process.

A second requirement is professional skill in analysing the reasons for student mistakes. Student errors are often superficial indicators of underlying misunderstandings or inadequately developed skills. There is no point creating the conditions for failure if there is no intention to investigate causes and provide feedback to guide learning. Skills of investigation and diagnosis are crucial to effective teaching and essential prerequisites for learning from mistakes.

CHAPTER 24

The hard work of improvement

NOVEMBER, 2011, *OCCASIONAL ESSAYS*, 'THE HARD WORK OF IMPROVEMENT' EXTRACT

In education it has been common to argue that teachers, as professionals, should be left alone to make their own judgements about appropriate teaching interventions and strategies. But it is interesting to contrast this argument with practice in other professions such as medicine where substantial work has been done to capture accumulated professional knowledge about best practice. Although professional judgement has an obvious place in the practice of medicine, there also are 'standards of care' that practitioners are expected to follow – agreed best practices for the handling and treatment of particular medical conditions based on accumulated professional experience.

Sustained, long-term improvements in educational outcomes similarly depend on studying, understanding, describing and promoting best practice throughout the profession. Such work goes well beyond mapping minimal expectations of schools, teachers and school leaders. It goes to the detail of highly effective teachers' pedagogical practices and highly effective leaders' day-to-day leadership work. It involves understanding the expert knowledge and skills that underlie best practice. And it probably involves the eventual development of 'standards of practice' – agreed best ways of professionally intervening and addressing particular kinds of educational problems and challenges.

Unlike the minimal expectations and compliance requirements of employers and governments, highly effective practices of this kind can be identified only through the systematic study of professional practice. What is it that expert mathematics teachers know and do that less able teachers do not? What are the distinguishing features of highly effective school leadership? What does it mean to become more expert in the assessment of student learning and the provision of effective feedback? The hard work of improvement begins with research-based understandings of the nature of excellent practice, whether of classroom teachers, school leaders or education systems.

And because excellence is developed incrementally over time, *quality metrics* always are based on a developmental view. They describe increasingly deep knowledge, understandings and practices in specific aspects of professional work, and so provide a framework for establishing where employees and organisations are at any given time in their ongoing development and what actions and learning may be required for further improvement.

Much is now known about what it means to become a more expert teacher. The development of pedagogical expertise includes becoming better at creating supportive learning environments in which all students are emotionally engaged and motivated to learn; establishing starting points for teaching by exploring where individuals are in their learning and development; making explicit to students what they are expected to learn; designing learning opportunities to address the needs of students who are at different points in their learning; connecting new material to past learning and assisting students to see continuity in their learning over time; promoting deep learning by emphasising underlying principles, concepts and big ideas; demonstrating explicitly what students are to do and checking that learning is occurring;

taking advantage of teaching and learning opportunities as they arise; providing ongoing feedback to students on their learning; and promoting positive student beliefs about their own capacity to learn.

Much is also known about the nature of school improvement. Schools usually become more effective places of learning by developing and implementing improvement strategies to which all staff are committed; systematically monitoring improvements in student outcomes and sharing this information across the school community; setting and communicating high expectations of all learners; identifying student needs and deploying staff and school resources in ways that best address those needs; creating a professional teaching team with high levels of subject knowledge and pedagogical expertise; ensuring whole-school curriculum clarity and vertical alignment to provide continuity of student learning across year levels; and promoting highly effective, evidence-based teaching practices throughout the school, including differentiated teaching to ensure that every student is engaged and learning successfully.

Studies of education systems that have achieved significant gains in student performance over time are providing insights into the nature of system improvement. These studies are suggesting that education systems become more effective by aligning effort at all levels of the system around the core goal of improving student learning. Such systems diagnose and study the details of student, school and system performance and target effort and resources on underperforming parts of the system. They build professional capacity by attracting more able people into teaching and by improving the effectiveness of initial and continuing teacher education, and they work to ensure that excellence is distributed throughout the system. High-performing education systems understand the essential importance of improving pedagogical practices and take a long-term perspective on changing the culture of the system – the values, understandings, skills, practices and relationships necessary for significantly enhanced performance (Fullan 2011).

Whether at the level of teachers and leaders, whole schools or entire systems, significant and sustained improvements in performance require more than a focus on results and more than compliance with standards and minimal expectations. The hard work of improvement requires deep engagement with the quality of practice.

In this context, research-based elaborations of what improving practice looks like – in the form of developmental frameworks and rubrics – provide quality metrics that enable individuals, organisations and systems to identify and reflect on current levels of practice, design improvement strategies and monitor improvements in their practice over time (Masters 2010).

Improved performances can be achieved by promoting greater attention to the results an organisation was established to deliver; by confirming that employees are performing the roles and tasks expected at their levels; and by ensuring organisational compliance with minimal standards of practice and behaviour. But deep and lasting improvements depend on studying and understanding highly effective professional practices and providing support and creating the conditions that make these practices part of ongoing day-to-day work.

> Editors' note: This extract is taken from the full-length paper 'The hard work of improvement', in which Masters examines the common strategies utilised by organisations to promote improved employee or organisational performance. The full text can be found at https://www.acer.org/occasional-essays/the-hard-work-of-improvement.

CHAPTER 25

Addressing the challenges

NOVEMBER, 2017, *REVIEW TO ACHIEVE EDUCATIONAL EXCELLENCE IN AUSTRALIAN SCHOOLS* SUBMISSION EXTRACT

The Australian Council for Educational Research (ACER) is engaged in research and development to address all four of these challenges in curriculum, assessment, teaching and reporting. We see this as difficult, long-term but essential work for improving outcomes in Australian schools. We also see this as a national agenda that would benefit from broad input and widespread collaboration.

In relation to the curriculum, in specific areas of learning we are working to develop and promote the concept of an underpinning continuum or 'progression' of learning that extends across the years of school. We have begun this work in the areas of reading and mathematics in collaboration with the UNESCO Institute for Statistics and with financial support from the Australian Department of Foreign Affairs and Trade. The reading and mathematics learning progressions we have developed are likely to provide a basis for the 'global metrics' that will be used internationally to monitor student learning and progress in achieving the UN's 2030 Sustainable Development Goal 4.1. These progressions and others we have begun developing in science, writing, creative thinking, critical thinking, collaboration and research skills are informed by empirical data on how progress occurs in each of these domains.

The learning progressions we are developing provide an alternative to presenting the curriculum as year-level 'packages' to be delivered to all students in the same year of school. Maps of long-term progress recognise that students of the same age/year level are at very different points in their learning and usually require different, well-targeted teaching and learning opportunities. They also provide a basis for monitoring long-term growth.

In relation to assessment, ACER now routinely designs assessment resources to establish where students are in their long-term learning progress. In other words, ACER assessments are aligned with, and locate students on, well-constructed learning progressions that describe the nature of development in particular areas of learning. For example, our Progressive Achievement (PAT) assessments, which are used online by the majority of Australian primary and secondary schools, allow teachers to administer different tests across the years of school, but provide information about where students are on the same underlying learning progressions in reading, mathematics and other aspects of literacy. The psychometric techniques that allow this approach are well developed and are being applied throughout ACER's assessment work.

Our current work includes the development of resources for teacher use in assessing skills in communicating, collaborating, critical thinking, creative thinking and research. These resources are based on complex problems on which students work in teams over a period of time. Each problem provides a context for making and recording observations relevant to this set of capabilities. A described and illustrated learning progression is being developed for each capability. At present, the focus is on assessing individuals, but this work is raising the question of whether useful assessments also could be made of the capabilities of teams.

In relation to teaching, ACER's starting point is to recognise that teachers generally teach subjects, and that highly effective teaching depends on expert content knowledge and pedagogical content knowledge within specific subjects. To maximise learning, teachers need to establish in some diagnostic detail where students are in their learning and then draw on their expert knowledge to promote further learning. This clinical approach to teaching requires a focus on subject-specific knowledge and strategies.

ACER's current work is focused on supporting teachers in their understanding and implementation of effective, evidence-based teaching of content and skills in learning areas such as mathematics, science, reading and writing. For example, following the assessment of students using our progressive achievement tests, our PAT Teaching Resources Centre provides teachers with targeted, subject-specific interventions and teaching strategies in reading and mathematics. Similarly, our work to support teachers to reflect on, and to provide evidence of, the effectiveness of their teaching uses portfolio entries based on subject-specific teaching (e.g. to develop students' capacities to write for a range of audiences and purposes; to build students' knowledge and conceptual understanding of important mathematics content through quality classroom discussion; and to develop students' skills in science inquiry). We focus on fine-grained, subject-specific teaching because we are convinced by the evidence that this is likely to be more effective in promoting successful learning than one-size-fits-all curriculum delivery, blanket teaching solutions or generic teaching standards.

In relation to reporting, we are working to develop and explore alternatives to A to E grades and other traditional forms of reporting. We are working on two fronts: to identify schools that are experimenting with improved ways of communicating and reporting learning to students and parents and carers; and to develop and explore improved ways of reporting learning against well-constructed learning progressions. This work is at an early stage, but we see it as crucial to reconceptualising curriculum, teaching, learning and assessment.

ACER recognises that there are many other challenges confronting school education in Australia, including challenges in the recruitment, training, deployment and ongoing development and recognition of teachers and school leaders. We see a number of these challenges as linked to the challenges outlined here. For example, the expectation that every student will make excellent progress every year has implications for how teachers and school leaders are deployed to schools in disadvantaged areas most in need of outstanding teaching and school leadership. A focus on student growth needs to become a fundamental element of all teacher preparation programs. The ability to diagnose student learning and to implement evidence-based, subject-specific teaching strategies and interventions needs to be a central goal of teacher professional development programs. And conceptualising and promoting teaching as professional work of this kind should make a contribution to raising the status of teaching and making it more attractive to more able school leavers.

ACER will continue its research and development efforts focused on reconceptualising school learning. It is clear that current approaches are not serving all students well – a fact reflected in the performance of Australian students in national and international achievement surveys. We believe that the challenges outlined here need to become a national agenda and a priority for governments and national education agencies. We stand ready to assist in the challenge of lifting achievement levels and improving the return on Australia's investment in schooling.

Editors' note: This extract is taken from the Australian Council for Educational Research's submission to the Panel for the *Review to Achieve Educational Excellence in Australian Schools,* chaired by Mr David Gonski AC. The full submission *Lifting achievement levels and improving return on Australia's investment in schooling* was submitted in November 2017. The submission observes that many students in Australian schools are not learning as well as they might because they are not being given learning opportunities at an appropriate level of challenge.

References

Ainley, J & Gebhardt, E 2013, *Measure for measure: a review of outcomes of school education in Australia*, ACER, Camberwell.

Australian Curriculum Assessment and Reporting Authority (ACARA) 2014, *National Assessment Program, Literacy and Numeracy – National report for 2014*, ACARA, Sydney.

Australian Institute for Teaching and School Leadership (AITSL) 2015, *Accreditation of initial teacher education programs in Australia – Standards and procedures*, AITSL, Melbourne.

Australian Research Alliance for Children and Youth (ARACY) 2007, *School readiness*, ARACY, West Perth.

Ausubel, DP 1968, *Educational psychology: a cognitive view*, Holt, Rinehart and Winston, New York.

Barber, M & Mourshed, M 2007, *How the world's best-performing schools come out on top*, McKinsey & Co., London.

Bloom, BS 1968, *Learning for mastery*, University of California Press, Los Angeles.

Boaler, J 2015, *What's math got to do with it? How teachers and parents can transform mathematics learning and inspire success*, Penguin Books, New York.

Bonnor, C & Shepherd, B 2014, *School equity: from bad to worse*, Inside Story, 22 October, viewed 5 September 2018, <https://insidestory.org.au/school-equity-from-bad-to-worse/>.

Bransford, JD, Brown, AL & Cocking, RR 1999, *How people learn: brain, mind, experience, and school*, National Academy Press, Washington.

Collarbone, P 2015, *Leading change, changing leadership (Part 2). System change moving to the next level of performance – incorporating two case studies*, Occasional paper 142, Centre for Strategic Education, East Melbourne.

Department of Education 2014, *Australian Early Development Census. 2012 Summary Report, November 2013*, Department of Education, Canberra.

Department of Education and Training 2018, *Report of the Review to Achieve*

Educational Excellence in Australian Schools, Commonwealth of Australia, Canberra.

Department of Education, Employment and Workplace Relations (DEEWR) 2009, *Belonging, being and becoming: the early years learning framework for Australia*, Commonwealth of Australia, Canberra.

Dweck, CS 2000, *Self-theories: their role in motivation, personality and development*, Psychology Press, Philadelphia.

Dweck, CS 2006, *Mindset: the new psychology of success*, Balantine Books, New York.

Early Childhood Australia 2011, *Early childhood education and care in Australia. A discussion paper prepared for the European Union–Australia policy dialogue*, Early Childhood Australia, Canberra.

Elliott, A 2006, *Early childhood education: pathways to quality and equity for all children*, Australian Education Review No. 50, ACER, Camberwell.

Frankl, V 1946, *Man's search for meaning*, Beacon Press, Boston.

Fullan, M 2011, *Choosing the wrong drivers for whole system reform*, Seminar series paper 204, May, Centre for Strategic Education, East Melbourne.

Griffin, P 2013, in J Topsfield, 'Results flatline for top students', *Age*, 10 January, viewed 5 September 2018, <https://www.theage.com.au/education/results-flatline-for-top-students-20130109-2cgud.html>.

Hanushek, EA 2002, *The failure of input-based schooling policies*, Working paper No. 9040, National Bureau of Economic Research, Cambridge, MA.

Hill, P & Barber, M 2014, *Preparing for a renaissance in assessment*, Pearson, London.

Hout, M & Elliott, SW (eds.) 2011, *Incentives and test-based accountability in education. Report of the Committee on Incentives and Test-Based Accountability in Public Education*. The National Academies Press, Washington.

Ko J, Sammons, P & Bakkum, L 2013, *Effective teaching: a review of research and evidence*, CfBT Education Trust, Reading.

Masters, G 2010, *Teaching and Learning School Improvement Framework*, ACER, Camberwell.

Masters, G 2011, *The power of expectation*, ACER Occasional Essays, October, ACER, Camberwell.

Masters, G 2011, *The hard work of improvement*, ACER Occasional Essays, November, ACER, Camberwell.

Masters, G 2012, *National School Improvement Tool*, ACER, Camberwell, viewed 5 September 2018, <https://research.acer.edu.au/cgi/viewcontent.cgi?article=1019&context=tll_misc>.

Masters, G 2013, *Reforming education assessment: imperatives, principles and challenges*, Australian Education Review No. 57, ACER, Camberwell, viewed 5 September 2018, <http://research.acer.edu.au/aer/12/>.

Masters, G 2013, *Towards a growth mindset in assessment*, ACER Occasional Essays, October, ACER, Camberwell.

Masters, G 2016, *Five challenges in Australian school education*, Policy Insights 5, ACER, Camberwell.

Masters, G 2016, *Schools as learning organisations*, ACER, Camberwell.

Muijs, D, Kyriakides, L, van der Werf, G, Creemers, B, Timperley, H & Earl, L 2014, 'State of the art: teacher effectiveness and professional learning', *School Effectiveness and School Improvement: An International Journal of Research, Policy and Practice*, vol. 25, pp. 231–256.

Organisation for Economic Co-operation and Development (OECD) 2011, *Building a high quality teaching profession: Lessons from around the world. Background report for the international summit on the teaching profession*, OECD, Paris.

Organisation for Economic Co-operation and Development (OECD) 2011, *Lessons from PISA for the United States. Strong performers and successful reformers in education*, OECD Publishing, Paris.

Organisation for Economic Co-operation and Development (OECD) 2013, *PISA 2012 results: excellence through equity. Giving every student the chance to succeed*, vol. II, PISA, OECD Publishing, Paris.

Otsuka, S & Smith, I 2005, 'Educational applications of the expectancy-value model of achievement motivation', *Change: Transformations in Education*, vol. 8 no. 1, pp. 91–109.

Pink, D 2009, *Drive: the surprising truth about what motivates us*, Riverhead Books, New York.

Pritchett, L & Beatty, A, 2012, *The negative consequences of overambitious curricula in developing countries*, Faculty Research Working Paper 12-035, John F Kennedy School of Government, Harvard, MA.

Rizzolatti, G & Fabbri-Destro, M 2010, 'Mirror neurons: from discovery to autism', *Experimental Brain Research*, vol. 200, nos. 3–4, pp. 223–37.

Rosenshine, B 2012, 'Principles of instruction: research-based principles that all teachers should know', *American Educator*, Spring 2012.

Sahlberg, P 2007, 'Education policies for raising student learning: the Finnish approach', *Journal of Education Policy*, vol. 22, no. 2.

Sahlberg, P 2010, *The secret to Finland's success: educating teachers*, Research Brief, Stanford Center for Opportunity Policy in Education, Stanford, CA.

Syed, M, 2015, *Black box thinking: the surprising truth about success (and why some people never learn from their mistakes)*, Hodder & Stoughton, London.

Thomson, S, De Bortoli, L & Buckley, S, 2013, *PISA 2012: How Australia measures up*, ACER, Camberwell.

Thomson, S; De Bortoli, L & Underwood, C 2017, *PISA 2015: Reporting Australia's results*, ACER, Camberwell, viewed 5 September 2018, <https://research.acer.edu.au/ozpisa/22>.

Thomson, S, Hillman, K, Schmid, M, Rodrigues, S, Fullarton, J 2017, *PIRLS 2016: Reporting Australia's results*, ACER, Camberwell, viewed 5 September 2018, <https://research.acer.edu.au/pirls/1/>.

Thomson, S, Hillman, K, Wernert, N, Schmid, M, Buckley, A & Munene, A, 2012, *Highlights from TIMSS & PIRLS 2011 from Australia's perspective*, ACER, Camberwell.

Thomson, S, Wernert, N, O'Grady, E, Rodrigues, S, 2016, *TIMSS 2015: Reporting Australia's results*, ACER, Camberwell, viewed 5 September 2018, <https://research.acer.edu.au/timss_2015/1>.

UNICEF 2012, *School readiness: a conceptual framework*, UNICEF, New York.

Vygotsky, L 1978, *Mind in society: the development of higher psychological processes*, eds & trans. M Cole, V John-Steiner, S Scribner & E Souberman, Harvard University Press, Cambridge, MA.

Weldon, PR 2015, *The teacher workforce in Australia: supply, demand and data issues*, Policy Insights 2, ACER, Camberwell.

World Bank 2010, *Europe and Central Asia Knowledge Brief*, The World Bank, Washington.

Index

A to E grades 70
  alternatives 131–2
ability 96
ability grouping 65–6
academic achievement *see* achievement
accountability 59
  questionable effectiveness 48
  strengthening to achieve higher standards 33
  systems 49
accreditation 10–11
achievement 13
  low achievement *see* underachievement
  minimum standards of 8, 32
  PISA findings 4, 21
  targeting to current levels of 37, 52
  value of high achievement 46–48
  variability 35, 79–80
achievement gaps 63–66
  group-based solutions 65
advantage 4
age-based teaching/learning approach 7
aging workforce 55
aptitude 15
assessment 45
  ACER resources design 130
  assessment *of* learning as vital work element 77
  challenges 99–100
  coming 'renaissance' 97
  'computer adaptive' 101
  designing the future 97–102
  diagnosing student learning situation 35, 43, 74–7
  failure to illuminate actual student variability 80–1
  formative and summative *see* formative assessment; summative assessment
  'formative' use of 77
  growth mindset in 86, 90–4
  of growth over time 90–2
  limited information provision 26
  new metrics 99–100
  new technologies 100–1
  new thinking 98–9
  perceptions 72
  purpose 70–2, 98
  reconceptualising 69–72, 75–102
  role, beliefs regarding 82
  understanding focus 98–9
  against year-level expectations, inadequacies 82
  year-level expectations influence on 7
  see also A to E grades
assessment reform 68–72
  pros and cons 71
  sub-fields 69
assessments *for* learning *see* formative assessment
assessments *of* learning *see* summative assessment
assumption
  regarding achievement 79
  regarding outcomes 62, 79
  same year–same readiness 85
ATAR bands
  growing teacher numbers drawn from lower 55–6
  objectives 13
  offers and percentages 11–12
attitude 15, 42
attributes 28–9, 84, 99–100
  broader range 31

INDEX

Australian Council for Educational Research (ACER), addressing challenges 129–32
Australian Curriculum
  age–school commencement mismatch 7
  an ageing curriculum? 5–6
  curriculum content 27, 29–30
  as potential progress 'map' 82
  shortcomings 5–7
Australian Early Development Census (AEDC) 39–40
  developmentally vulnerable children, monitoring 40
Australian perspectives
  academic decline by comparison 6, 17
  Education offers–ATARs proposed objective 13
  high international levels – reading and mathematics 78–9
  increased number of teachers required over next decade 54
  international baseline proficiency level 32–4
  middle third of school leavers as teacher 'bank' debate 3, 10–14
  research contributions and STEM specialists 26
  between-school variance 17–23
  socioeconomic gap (schools) 5, 17
Australian schools, reducing inter-school disparity 5–6, 18–24
Australian Tertiary Admission Rank (ATAR) 10–13

beliefs 82–3, 95–6, 123
best practice 65, 125–6
between-school variance 4–5, 17–23
  education policy decisions changing 20–1
  objectives 20
  policies reducing impact of 21–2
  versus 'within-school' 19

capability variations 79–80
Centre for Assessment Reform and Innovation (CARI) 97
change
  global accelerated pace of 5
  marginal political response to 2
  pedagogical change 27
  'revolutionary' change *versus* 'evolutionary' change 109
chemistry 53, 55
children
  developmentally vulnerable 39–41
  good start 39–44
  at-risk 8–9, 39–40

children's needs *see* learning needs
chunking 85
coaching 3
cognitive and/or non-cognitive 'deficits' 41, 43
collaboration 43, 100, 105–9, 129–30
comfort zone 36, 81, 117
common curriculum 72
Commonwealth Government 55
  grading 83, 93
communication 5, 13, 27, 56, 84, 99, 114, 130
community 114
composite classes 7, 34
continuous improvement 53, 113
  school improvement cycle 105–9
courses
  delivery and learning 27, 68, 117, 119–20
  deriving learning position without accessing 74–5
  group delivery 117
  limited and competitive 3, 10–15
creative thinking 129–30
creativity 26
critical thinking 15, 99, 129–30
cross-curricular skills 6, 99–100
culture
  intercultural understanding 99–100
  learning culture 123–4
  stronger performance cultures 58
  that accepts mistakes 121
  that promotes learning 112
curricula
  advanced STEM curriculum 28
  all-age appropriateness 7, 35, 81–2
  alternative belief system 84–5
  for Australian schools *see* Australian Curriculum
  'crowded' 30
  failure to illuminate actual student variability 79–80
  one-size-fits-all curriculum delivery 131
  questionable preparation for life/work 26–7
  systematic curriculum delivery 113
  whole-school curriculum clarity 127
  year-level 79, 80–1
curricular gap 80
curriculum design
  for the 21st century 5–6
  breadth–depth balance consideration 29–30
curriculum priorities
  cross-disciplinary, team-based problem solving promotion 30–1
  depth not breadth of learning 29–30

data analysis and discussion 112
'deficits' 41, 43
demographics 63, 65
'developmental continua' 92
developmental delays 8, 39
   early detection 43
developmental frameworks 128
developmental vulnerability 40–2
differentiated learning 113
differentiated teaching 71, 84, 113, 118
digital assessments 101
direct incentives 48–49
disadvantage 4, 8, 39, 42, 132
   reducing impact of 21–2
disengagement 33, 39, 80
dropping out 80

early childhood education and care, quality 42–3
early intervention 47
education
   focus on larger purpose of schooling 61–2
   further 15, 47–8
   high quality 17, 47–8
   organisation and delivery contributing to underperformance 78–82
   skills of learning from mistake 123–4
   value of 46
Education offers 11–12
educational assessment *see* assessment
educational challenges 2–44
educational outcomes 40, 62
   different outcomes, different solutions assumption 62
   measuring and monitoring improvements 107
   streaming by ability/repeating and 79
   see also learning outcomes
educational performance 53
employers, information needs 26
end-of-course examinations 77
engagement, positive 42
environment
   competitive 27
   environmental challenges 24
   safe, respectful, tolerant, inclusive 112
   technology-enhanced 101
equity 62, 71
   equitable resource distribution 4, 22–3
   improving 39
   versus learning needs continuum 36
errors/mistakes 116
   learning from mistakes 121–4

evaluation
   essential element 77
   general approaches 90–4
   of past progress 76
   strategy effectiveness 98
evidence gathering 100
evidence-based practices 23, 65, 127, 131–2
expectations 71
   consistent 113
   couched in terms of student *progress* 71
   of excellent learning progress 47–48
   excellent progress 86
   living up to high or low 96
   minimal 125–6, 128
   parental 95
   power of expectation 95–6
   set when grouped by ability or labelled 65–6
   year-level *see* year-level expectations
expenditure
   educational expenditure–performance link (PISA) 4
   increases 57
explicit instruction 114

families 110, 112, 113, 114
   school reports sharing progress 37–8
feedback 90–4, 115, 122–3
   immediate feedback to guide action 118–19
   planned and episodic 118–19
   quality of 119
financial rewards 49, 58
   sometimes counterproductive 60
formative assessment 69–70, 115
   describing particular use of assessment information 76
   rethinking 74–7
   summative–formative distinction 76–7
'free time' (reward) 81
funding
   funding policies 5
   levels 61

gender mix 55, 63
general capabilities 99–100
generalist primary teachers 54
'global metrics' 129
globalisation 5
government(s) 57
   influence on assessment perception 72
   residualisation-changing policy 21
   teacher recruitment aspirations 12–14

group-specific educational solutions 64–5
growth
    assessing over time 90–2
    learning focus 6–7
    monitoring student growth 84–9
growth mindset 85–6, 90–4

improvement 125–8
    improvement agenda, explicit 111–12
    strategy 108
    see also continuous improvement
incentives 48–9
    an ineffective school improvement strategy? 57–60
Index of Community Socio-Educational Advantage (ICSEA), school groupings 18
Indigenous children 61–2, 63–5
    disadvantage, multiple forms of 8, 39–40
individuality/individuals 63, 67, 70–2, 83, 86, 88, 89, 90–4, 113, 116–18
    individualised support 44
    tailoring teaching to meet individual needs 117–18
information
    access to 5
    essential 98
    systematic and reliable collection of 106
    usable 72
initiatives 58
innovation 5, 51, 78–9
    innovative solutions 26, 31
instructional courses *see* courses
intercultural understanding 99
international baseline proficiency level 32, 34
International Conference on Giftedness and Talent Development 79
international perspectives
    deliberate and sustained public policies 46–8
    educational expenditure 4
    high international levels – reading and mathematics 78–9
    high-performing teacher education systems 3
    international programs *see* Programme for International Student Assessment; Trends in International Mathematics and Science Study
    OECD baseline proficiency estimates 32, 34
    between-school variance 4–5, 17–23
    student selection mechanisms 15
    top-performing nations 3, 10–16
intervention 47
intervention strategies 43

investigation 122–4

key performance indicators (KPIs), national 12–14, 19–20, 27–9, 34, 40–4
knowledge
    expert content knowledge 131
    explosion of 5
    factual and procedural emphasis 5–6, 26, 30
    subject-specific knowledge 131
    transfer to unfamiliar contexts 30
knowledge economies 79

labels 65–6
language teaching 53
leaders/leadership
    high quality and equitably distributed leadership 21–2
    maximised access to 21–2
learners
    ascertaining what learner already knows 80–1
    assisting to see and appreciate progress 119–20
    establishing where learners are in their progress 116–17
    as 'good'/'poor' thinking 92
    inherently poor 33, 72, 92
    perceptions 83
    personal goals and motivations 116
    progress (or growth) re-definition 36–7
learning
    chunking 85
    continuous workplace learning 5
    current individual focus 6
    equating high grades with successful learning 81–3
    fear of blame (undermining) 122
    growth 84–9
    on the job 29
    from mistakes 121–4
    monitoring over time 36–7
    ongoing 9, 15
    organisation approach 7, 37–8
    passive, reproductive learning emphasis 26
    perceptions 83
    personalised 36, 71
    progress over the year *versus* progress as against others 36–8
    reconceptualising 'success' 36–8
    willingness to learn 13, 122
learning arrangements, flexible 6–7
learning assessment, designing the future 97–102
learning culture 123–4

learning difficulties, school-entry diagnosis 9
learning domains
　AEDC domains 40
　core concepts – 'big ideas' 30
　mapping 86–9
　real-world contexts 24–6
　segregated, isolated and non-interactive 4–5, 26–7
　what long-term growth looks like 92
learning environments, isolated and competitive in nature 27
learning frameworks 92
learning needs 8–9
　addressing 39
　diagnosis of learning position 35, 43, 52, 74–5
　flexible solutions to meet 6–7
　identifiable but similar learning needs in groups 64
　identifying and meeting 8–9
　individual 9
　meeting on school entry 42
　special 8
　tailoring teaching to meet 117–8
　workplace learning requirement 5
learning opportunities 71, 83, 122, 126–7, 130
　appropriate (well-targeted) 66
learning organisations, schools as 103–33
learning outcomes
　assessment *for* improved learning outcomes 75
　dependence on knowledge of achievement 36
　determinants 27
learning readiness 35
　targeting to current levels of 36, 52
legislation
　age-based approach enforcement 7
　grading against year-level curriculum expectations 82, 93
　No Child Left Behind (US) 58
literacy 10–11, 15, 56, 61, 64, 130
　declining levels of 'literacy' 17, 24–5, 28
　monitoring via survey *see* Programme for International Student Assessment
　national 27–9
'literacy' perspective 99

mapping 86–9, 125
　advantages 88
marginalisation 37–8
master's degree 47
mathematics 53–4, 78–9
　achievement differences 8–9

OECD baseline proficiency level estimates 32
　popularity decline 6, 24–5
　20-year slide 50–2
McKinsey study
　policies driving improvement 14–16
　of school systems 12, 13–16
measure of success 28
mentoring 3
metrics
　'global metrics' 129
　new metrics 99–100
　quality metrics 126, 128
mindset 85–6, 89, 90–4
　'fixed mindset' 204
　'growth mindset for schools' 104
　operating in tandem 93–4
mixed-ability classes 7, 34, 79

National Assessment Program Literacy and Numeracy (NAPLAN) 8
　reading results 18
National Partnership Agreement on Universal Access to Early Childhood Education 42
National Quality Framework 42
National Research Council (US) 60
National School Improvement Tool (the Tool) 107, 110–14
　nine interrelated 'domains' 111–14
　see also continuous improvement
neuroscience 95
new metrics 99–100
new technologies 100–01
new thinking 98–99
numeracy 10–11, 15, 56
　decline 17

observation 74, 130
Organisation for Economic Co-operation and Development (OECD) 4–5, 15–16, 17, 20–3, 24, 27–28
　baseline proficiency level estimates 32, 34
　resource expenditure, and distribution of 4, 22–3
　see also Programme for International Student Assessment

parents
　expectations 95
　sharing learning progress 37–8
　student progress information 93
　see also families
participation rates 25

INDEX

part-time employment 55
pay-for-results 60
pedagogy
  changes 27
  effective pedagogical practices 43, 113–14, 125
  pedagogical expertise 127–8
peers, student groupings 7, 34, 79–80
performance
  ATAR indicators 10–13
  Australian decline as against other countries 7, 16
  performance pay 58
  PISA's between-school variance 4–5
  real-time 101
  top-performing nations 3, 12
  'value-added' measures of 58
  year-level expectations factoring into assessment of 8
  see also achievement; underachievement
performance gap 50, 78–9
personality 15
physics 25, 53–4, 55, 74
plans/planning
  planned and episodic feedback 118–19
  planned programs of support 44
  planning a stronger teacher workforce 53–6
  planning future action (in light of where students are at, learning-wise) 75
  school improvement plan 105–9
policy, procedure, protocol
  effective policies 14–16, 20–3
  funding policies 5
  'input-based' policies 57
  policies reducing between-school disparities 21–2
  policy response to underachievement 33
  policy settings' effect on reform 48–50
  quick-fix marginal change 2
  residualisation-changing policy 21
  school-wide policies, practices and programs 112
  student streaming policies 21
practices
  parental 42
  professional *see* professional practice
prejudice 63
preschool years 42–3
priorities, curriculum priorities 29–31
problem solving 5, 6, 15, 29, 84
  in real-world contexts 6, 24–6, 99
  standard problem types 26
  team-based 30–1
professional development, rigorous initial and continuing 15

professional experience placements 15
professional practice
  best practice 65
  effective pedagogical practices 113–14
  essential teaching practices, existence 115–20
  evidence-based practices 23
  implications of paradigm shift 69
  informed 116
  parallels 116
  professional capacity 129–30
  school improvement practices 23
  'standards of care' 125
  see also best practice
'proficiency scales' 92
Programme for International Student Assessment (PISA) 4, 16, 17, 23, 24
  literacy monitoring 27–8
  between-school variance 4–5, 19–21
Progressive Achievement (PAT) assessments 88, 130, 131
psychometric techniques 130

quality imperative
  early childhood education and care 42–3
quality metrics 126, 128

RAND Education 60
reading
  achievement differences 8
  change in average reading levels 59
  NAPLAN reading results (ICSEA grouped) 18
  OECD baseline proficiency level estimates 32
  reading proficiency 'map' 87–9
real-world contexts, fundamental concepts and principles application in 24–6
recruitment
  government aspirations for 12–13
  rankings and offerings *see* Australian Tertiary Admission Rank
  selection methods/processes 3, 10–13
reflection 76–7, 108–9
reform 46–66
  policy settings can make a difference 46–8
  right drivers identification 48–9
relationships
  between effort and success 87, 91–5
  influences of 43
  positive and caring relationships 112
  between student performance and socioeconomic status 4
remedial teaching 47

remuneration 15
repeating (school years) 79
reports/reporting
   alternative reporting formats 72
   alternatives to current reporting practices 93
   arguments for traditional forms 71–2
   perceptions 83
   school reports sharing progress 37–8
research 79, 129–32
   classroom-based 47
   doubt regarding incentives theoretical underpinnings 59–60
   research contributions and STEM specialists 26
   research-based dissertation 47
   on school leadership teams 111
residualisation 21, 23
resilience 122
resources 114
   ACER resources design 130
   distribution 4, 23
   targeted use of school resources 112
rewards, 'free time' as 81
risk, at-risk children 8–9, 39–40
rubrics 128

salary 15
sanctions 60
school community 114
school education *see* education
school improvement cycle
   current situation 106
   designing and implementing improvement strategy 107
   measuring and monitoring improvements in outcomes 107
   reflecting on what has been learned 108–9
   specifying desired outcome improvements 106
school improvement plan 106
school improvement practices 22
school leadership teams 110, 111
school leavers 3, 10–11
school readiness 9, 43
school reform *see* reform
school systems 47, 124–5, 129
   closing gaps 61–2
   consistently high standards challenge 20
   'equitable' 62
   Finland's publicly-funded 20
   influence on assessment perception 72
   McKinsey study of 12, 14–15
school–community partnerships 114
schools
   Australian 4–5
   children 'unready' for 41
   dropping out 80
   ICSEA-based groupings 18
   as learning organisations 104–32
   less 'attractive' 22
   raising the bar 33
   smooth transitions into 42–4
   unintended and undesirable behaviours 60
science
   popularity decline 6, 24–5
   20-year slide 50–2
science, technology, engineering and mathematics (STEM) 26, 51
   importance 28
secondary school 50–51, 54–55
   curriculum influences 6
   gender mix 57
   streaming into 19–20
   subject achievement information 26
segregation, based on socioeconomic background 4
self-confidence 37, 92, 95
self-management 99, 100
skills 13, 14, 27, 45, 56, 84, 86, 88–9, 91, 97, 122, 124, 125
   for the 21st century 6, 24, 99–100
   broader range 30–1
   deficits 36
   general 28–9
   not yet mastered 116
   science, technology, engineering and mathematics (STEM) skills 26
social networks 5
societal challenges 24, 26, 64
society, values placed on education and high achievement 46–8
socioeconomic context 4, 8, 17–18, 20–1, 39–40, 61–2, 63–6
   widening Australian socioeconomic schools gap 5
specialist support 44, 56
stakeholders 71
standards 128
   higher 33
   judge-and-grade requirement 33
   organisational compliance 128
   standards of care 125–6
Standing Council on School Education and Early Childhood (SCSEEC) 110
strategy 34–8, 41–4, 48–9, 57–60, 127–8, 131–2
   effectiveness 98

improvement strategy 107
student engagement, determinants 27
student residualisation 21
student streaming 19–21, 47, 66, 79
students
   assignation to groups 7, 34, 63–6
   beliefs about own abilities 96
   challenging 78–83
   'distance travelled' (success definition) 92
   learning from student mistakes 124
   learning position, establishing 9, 35, 43, 52, 74–5
   monitoring learning growth 84–9
   'peer' groupings 7, 34, 79–80
   raising the bar 33
   role, beliefs regarding 82
   school–work experiential divide 6, 27
   what students know, understand and can do 74
student-teacher ratios 61
summative assessment 68–70
   providing coarse rather than fine diagnostic detail 76
   rethinking 74–7
   summative–formative distinction 76–7
support
   planned programs of 44
   remedial support 118

targeted teaching 83
   starting points 98
teacher capacities 47
teacher education
   growing numbers drawn from lower ATAR bands 55–6
   highly selective programs 14–15
   limited and competitive courses 3, 10–12
   screening, testing and interviewing applicants 15
teachers
   broad repertoire of teaching methods 115
   deep understanding of nature of long-term learning progress 84
   drawn from school leavers 3, 10–11
   establishing diagnostic detail 131
   increased number required over next decade 54
   learning from student mistakes 124
   less effective teachers moved to less 'attractive' schools 22
   maximised access to quality teachers and leaders 21–2
   oversupply of 54
   pool of registered teachers 54
   raising status of 2–4, 10–16
   raising the bar 33
   roles 82, 116–17
   supply and demand control 14–15, 53–5
   undersupply of 53
   unintended and undesirable behaviours of 60
   workforce changes 55
teaching
   assessing learning position prior to 35, 43
   essential teaching practices, existence 115–20
   missing the mark 80
   motivation for 13
   organisation approach 7
   'out-of-field' 53–4, 82–3
   perceptions 83
   personalised 36
   raising effectiveness of 51
   subject-specific teaching 131
   tailoring to meet individual needs 117–18
   targeted 36, 52, 83
   value and competitiveness of 14–15
teaching profession
   as career choice 2–3, 10, 13–14
   entry comparisons 13
   a knowledge-based profession 10
   placements 15
   raising status of 2–4, 10–16
   status-raising policies for 14–16
Teaching Resources Centre 131
teams/teamwork
   cross-disciplinary 30–1
   expert teaching team 113
   multi-disciplinary 5
   school leadership teams 111
   workplace organisation around 27
technology
   advances 5, 29, 36, 97, 100
   new technologies 100–1
   technology-enhanced environments 101
   transforming course delivery and learning 27
test results transparency 58
thinking, new 98–9
Tomorrow's Schools program (NZ) 58
trajectories (of low achievement) 8–9, 39, 41
transparency 58
trends
   declining performance 4
   downward 13, 16
   evidence of 107
   low ATAR entry 55–6
   reversal 5–6, 13, 16, 28
   static performance–socioeconomic background

relationship 4
Trends in International Mathematics and Science Study (TIMSS) 50

underachievement
   'long tail' of 8–9, 32–8, 39–40
   policy response to 33
underperformance 79–83
understandings 29–31
   of concepts and principles 99
   versus 'judging' 91
   over time 85–6

visualisation 95

wellbeing 112, 114
willingness to learn 13, 122–4
work
   on-the-job learning 26
   knowledge-based 5
workforce
   changes 55
   mobility 5
   planning a stronger teacher workforce 53–6
workplaces
   continuous learning for 5
   organisation around teamwork 27

Year 3, achievement differences 8, 39
Year 8 50, 78
Year 12
   advanced subjects studies, decline in 3, 24–5, 28
   ATAR band offers and percentages 11–13
year-level curricula 79, 80–1
year-level expectations 7–8, 72, 80–3
   children well behind 8, 39
   explicit national requirement 33
   versus reality (being years ahead/behind) 80–3, 85
   versus student's excellence expectations 7

zone of proximal development (ZPD) (Vygotsky) 36, 81, 117

www.ingramcontent.com/pod-product-compliance
Lightning Source LLC
Chambersburg PA
CBHW051409070526
44584CB00023B/3358